This book is a collaboration between
Fondation Ipsen and Mayo Clinic.

The story has been inspired by
Golden Ella's experience with sickle cell disease.

The words in bold refer to key terms on page 32.

MEDICAL EDITOR

Asmaa Ferdjallah, M.D., M.P.H., Senior Associate Consultant, Division of Pediatric Hematology/Oncology, Mayo Clinic, Rochester, MN; Assistant Professor of Pediatrics, Mayo Clinic College of Medicine and Science

SERIES CONCEPTION

Fredric B. Meyer, M.D., Consultant, Department of Neurologic Surgery, Mayo Clinic, Rochester, MN; Executive Dean of Education, Professor of Neurosurgery, Mayo Clinic College of Medicine and Science

James A. Levine, M.D., Ph.D., Professor, President, Fondation Ipsen, Paris, France

My Life Beyond
SICKLE CELL DISEASE

A Mayo Clinic patient story
by Hey Gee and Golden Ella

MAYO CLINIC PRESS KIDS

Foreword

Hi!

My name is Golden Ella, and sickle cell disease has been a part of my life since I was 9 months old. I was already walking, and my mom and dad say I was a chubby-cheeked, curious, lively, smart and friendly baby girl. Suddenly, I became very ill, with a lot of pain in my hips and joints. I stopped walking and was listless, on my back, not able to even lift my arms and legs. I went to the emergency room and was hospitalized. I had osteomyelitis, an infection of the hipbones. That's when we found out I have sickle cell disease.
My hipbone infection was a complication of the disease. I had surgery and several infusions, and unending clinic and hospital visits. It was a revolving door.

However, I, for one, have decided sickle cell disease should not stop me from being my vivacious, vibrant and versatile self! I am a dancer and a Lego robotics programmer, builder and competitor. I like coding and computer programming. I am in drama and honors choir too. I sing my heart out! And I run track and field, holding my own even when I tire easily. I am doing my best to live life to its fullest potential. I hope to become a pediatric hematologist/oncologist, like the specialist doctor I see, and find a cure for sickle cell disease.

As you read this book, I hope you find the courage to lift yourself up and live your life to its fullest potential. If you have sickle cell disease, it does not need to define your amazing future. Stay positive! Be your vivacious, versatile and can-do self. Wishing you a healthful life journey.

Peace, love and health,
Golden Ella

"
NOTHING IS IMPOSSIBLE
"

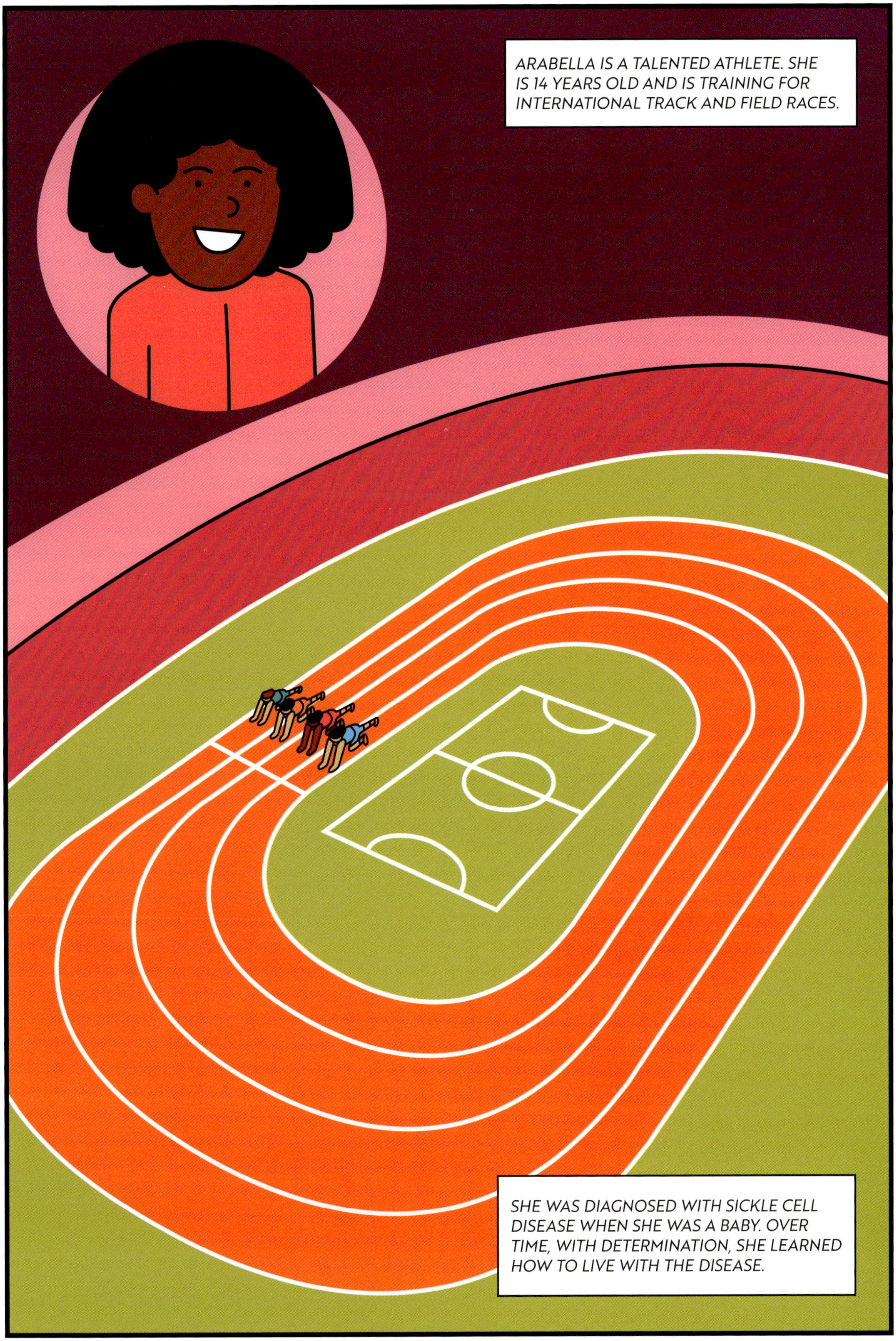
ARABELLA IS A TALENTED ATHLETE. SHE IS 14 YEARS OLD AND IS TRAINING FOR INTERNATIONAL TRACK AND FIELD RACES.
SHE WAS DIAGNOSED WITH SICKLE CELL DISEASE WHEN SHE WAS A BABY. OVER TIME, WITH DETERMINATION, SHE LEARNED HOW TO LIVE WITH THE DISEASE.

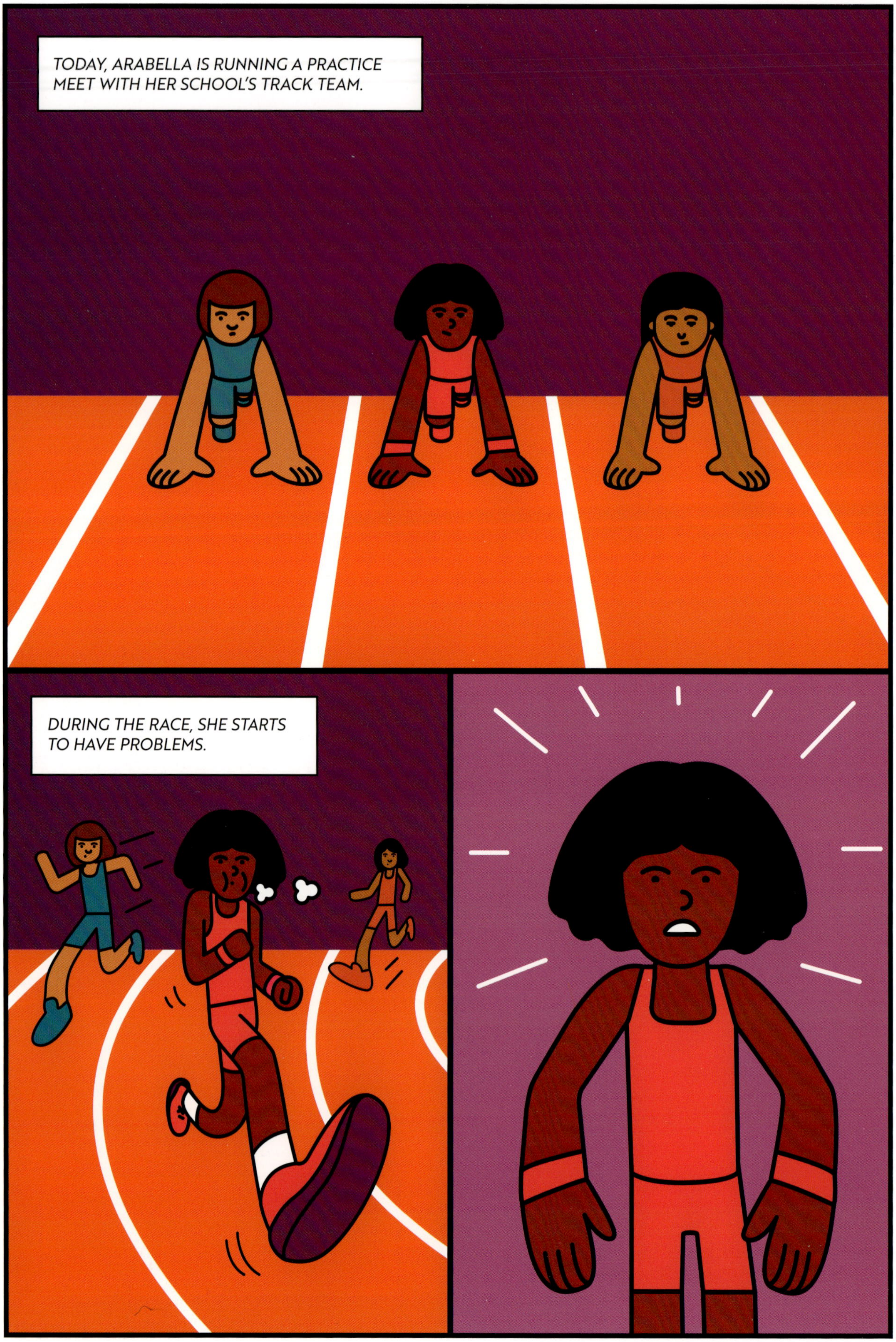
TODAY, ARABELLA IS RUNNING A PRACTICE MEET WITH HER SCHOOL'S TRACK TEAM.
DURING THE RACE, SHE STARTS TO HAVE PROBLEMS.

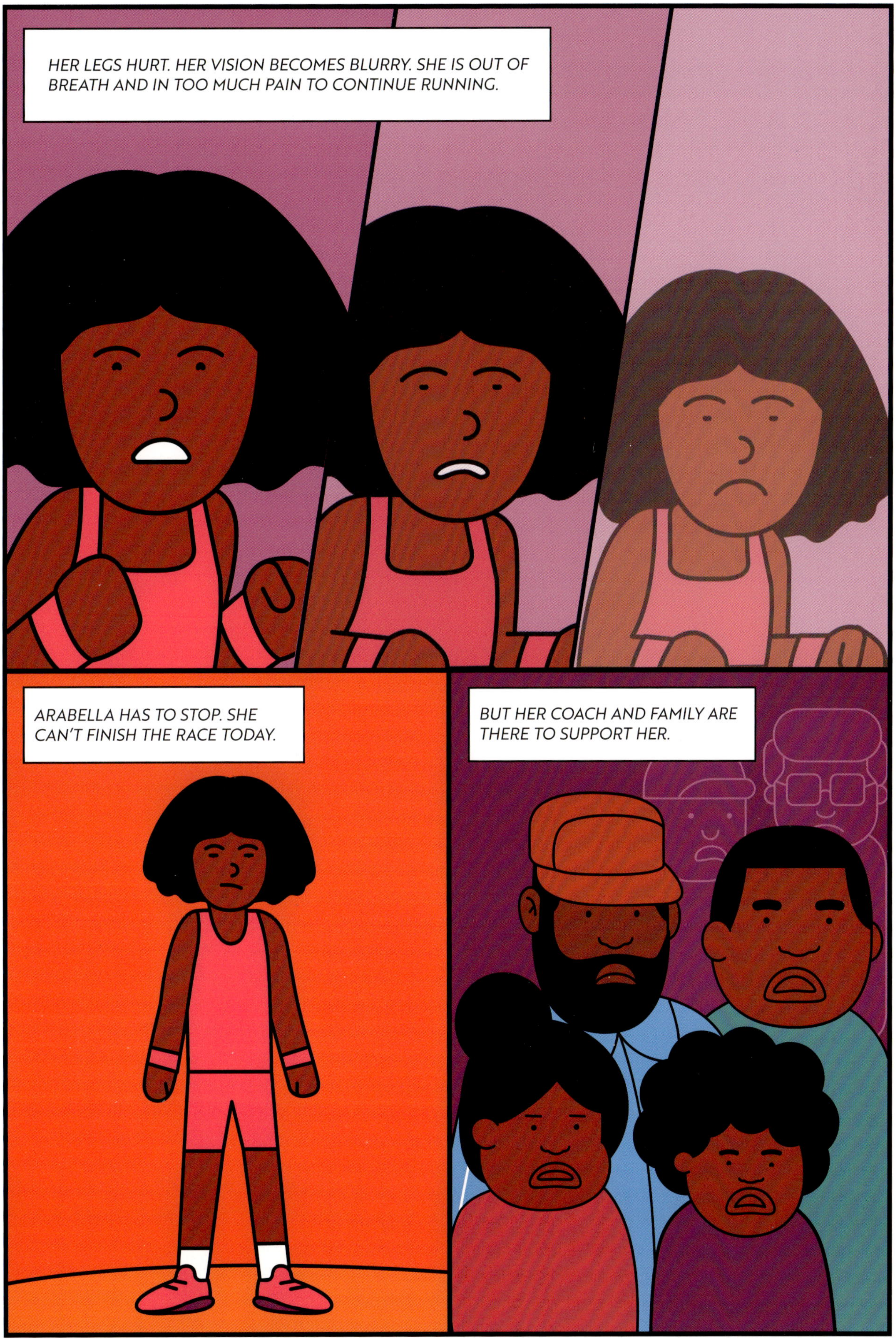
HER LEGS HURT. HER VISION BECOMES BLURRY. SHE IS OUT OF BREATH AND IN TOO MUCH PAIN TO CONTINUE RUNNING.
ARABELLA HAS TO STOP. SHE CAN'T FINISH THE RACE TODAY.
BUT HER COACH AND FAMILY ARE THERE TO SUPPORT HER.

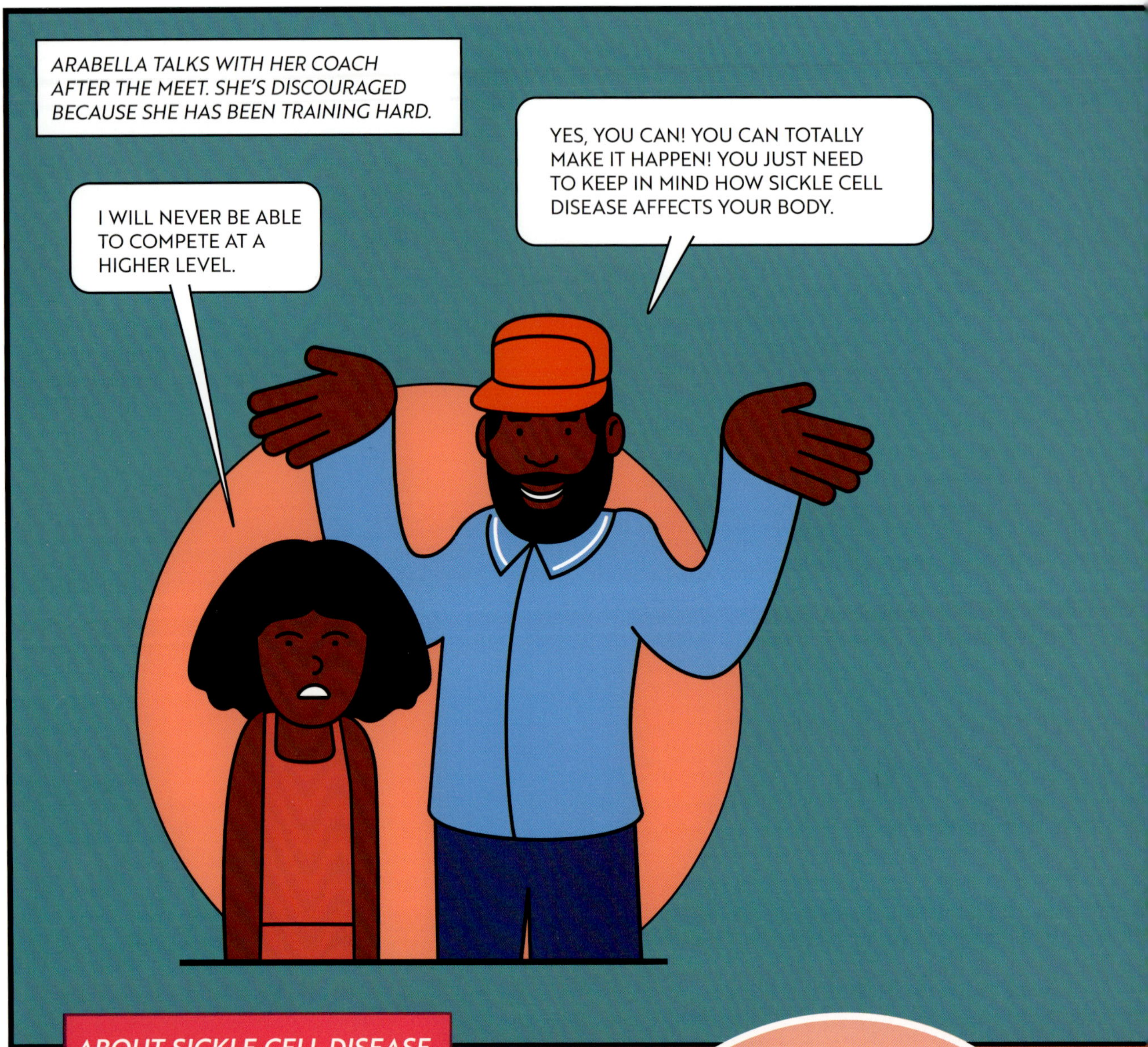
ARABELLA TALKS WITH HER COACH AFTER THE MEET. SHE'S DISCOURAGED BECAUSE SHE HAS BEEN TRAINING HARD.
I WILL NEVER BE ABLE TO COMPETE AT A HIGHER LEVEL.
YES, YOU CAN! YOU CAN TOTALLY MAKE IT HAPPEN! YOU JUST NEED TO KEEP IN MIND HOW SICKLE CELL DISEASE AFFECTS YOUR BODY.

ABOUT SICKLE CELL DISEASE

*SICKLE CELL DISEASE AFFECTS **RED BLOOD CELLS** THAT CARRY OXYGEN THROUGHOUT THE BODY. HEALTHY **RED BLOOD CELLS** ARE ROUND AND FLEXIBLE. BUT WITH SICKLE CELL DISEASE, SOME OF THESE CELLS BECOME STIFF AND STICKY AND SHAPED LIKE CRESCENT MOONS, ALSO CALLED SICKLE-SHAPED.*

THEY EASILY GET STUCK IN SMALL BLOOD VESSELS. THIS CAN SLOW OR BLOCK THE FLOW OF BLOOD AND OXYGEN AROUND THE BODY.

*SICKLE CELL DISEASE CAUSES **ANEMIA. ANEMIA** IS WHEN A PERSON DOES NOT HAVE ENOUGH HEALTHY **RED BLOOD CELLS** TO CARRY OXYGEN THROUGHOUT THE BODY. **ANEMIA** CAN CAUSE TIMES OF EXTREME PAIN CALLED PAIN CRISES.*

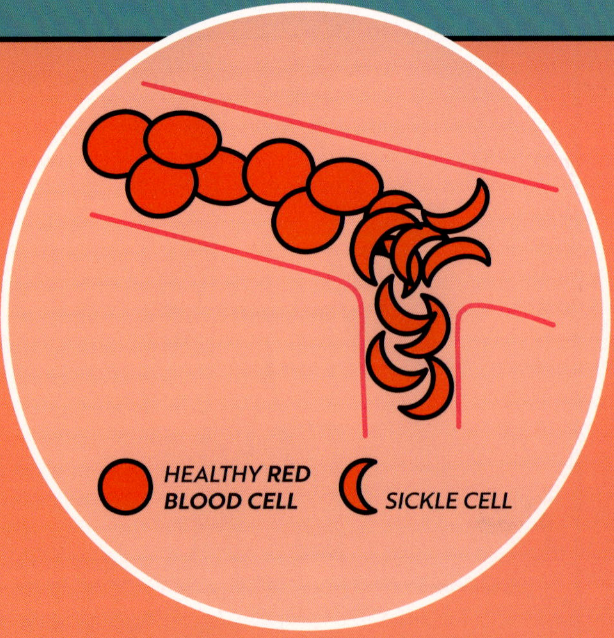
HEALTHY RED BLOOD CELL
SICKLE CELL

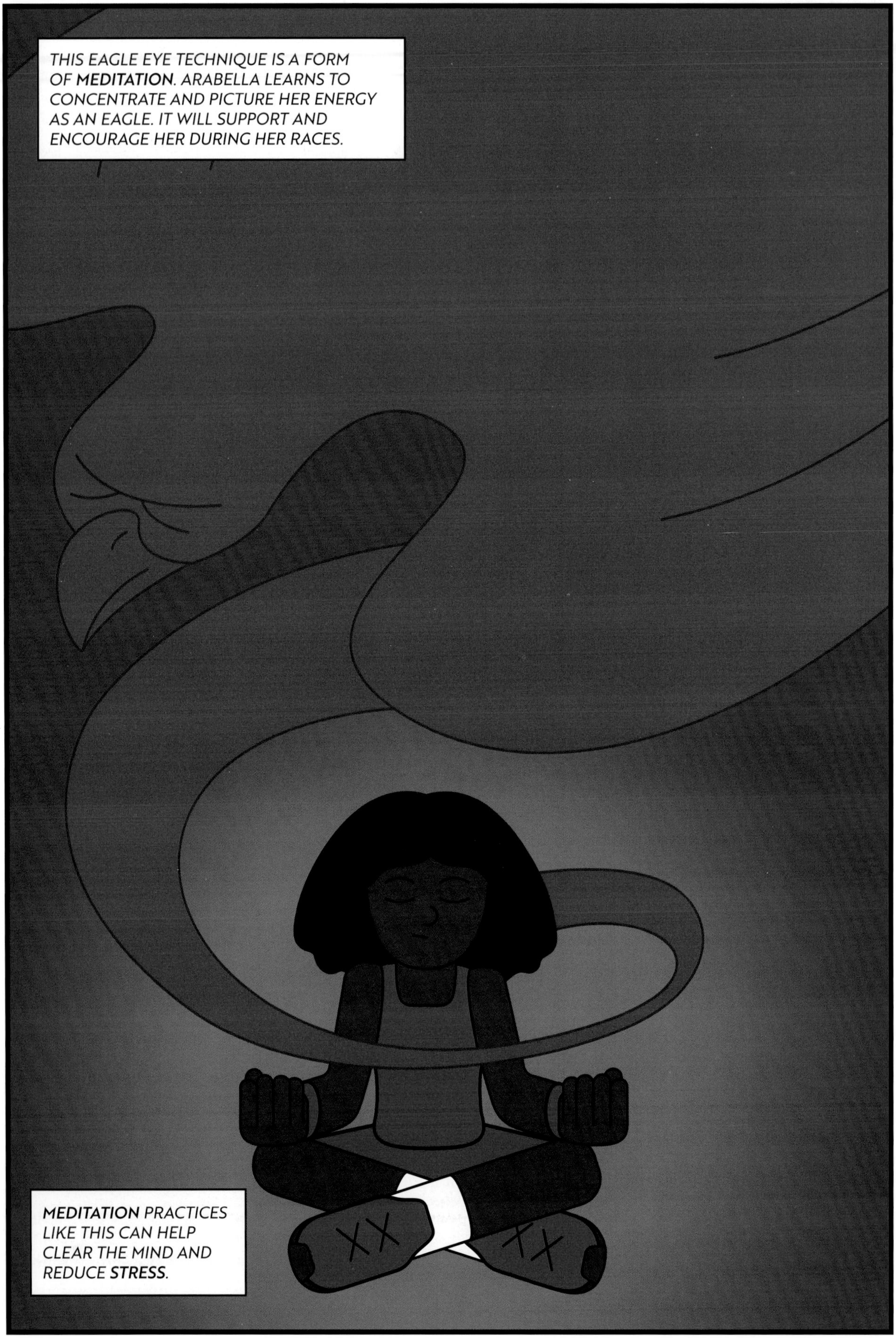
THIS EAGLE EYE TECHNIQUE IS A FORM OF **MEDITATION**. ARABELLA LEARNS TO CONCENTRATE AND PICTURE HER ENERGY AS AN EAGLE. IT WILL SUPPORT AND ENCOURAGE HER DURING HER RACES.
MEDITATION PRACTICES LIKE THIS CAN HELP CLEAR THE MIND AND REDUCE **STRESS**.

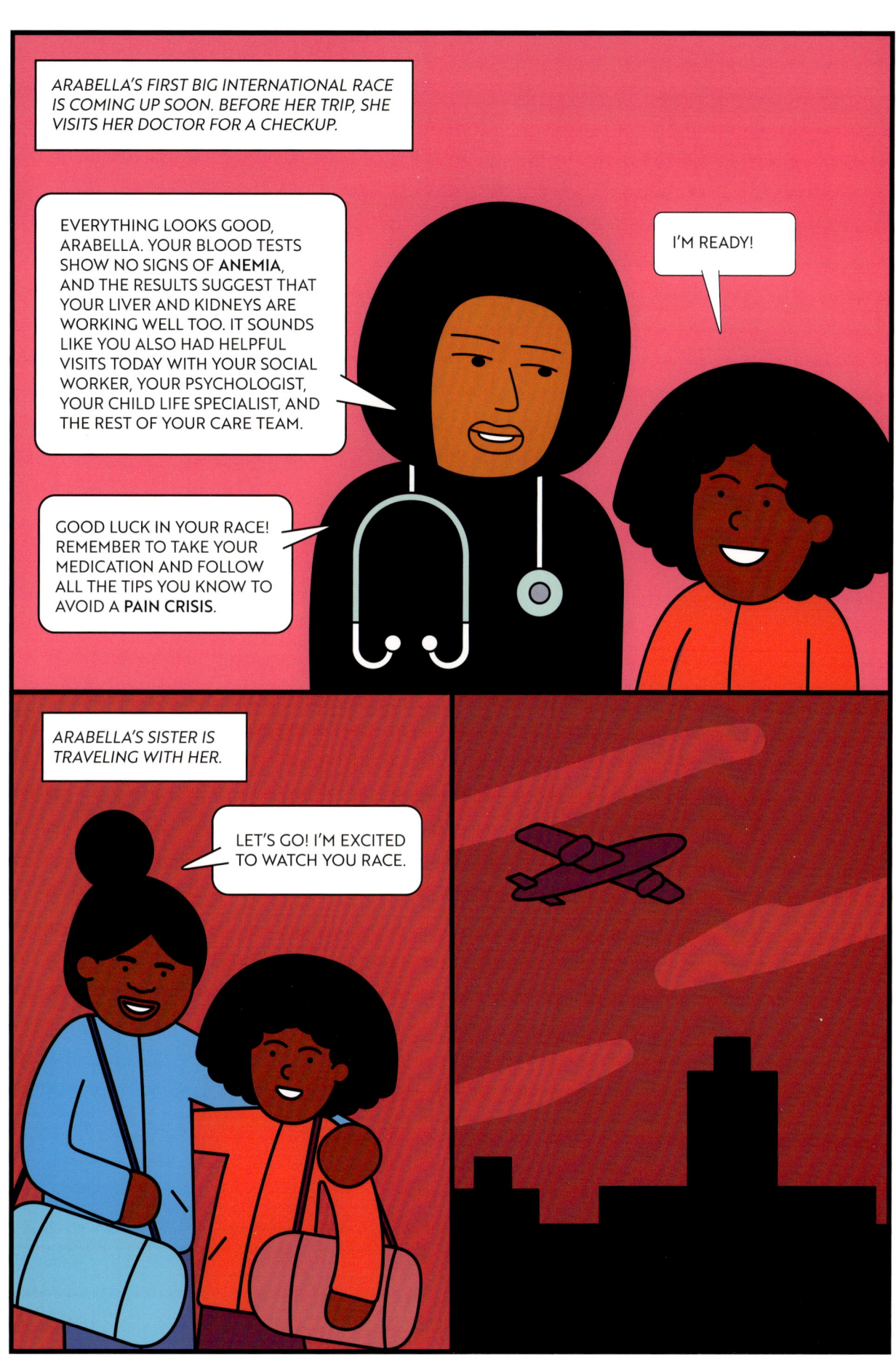

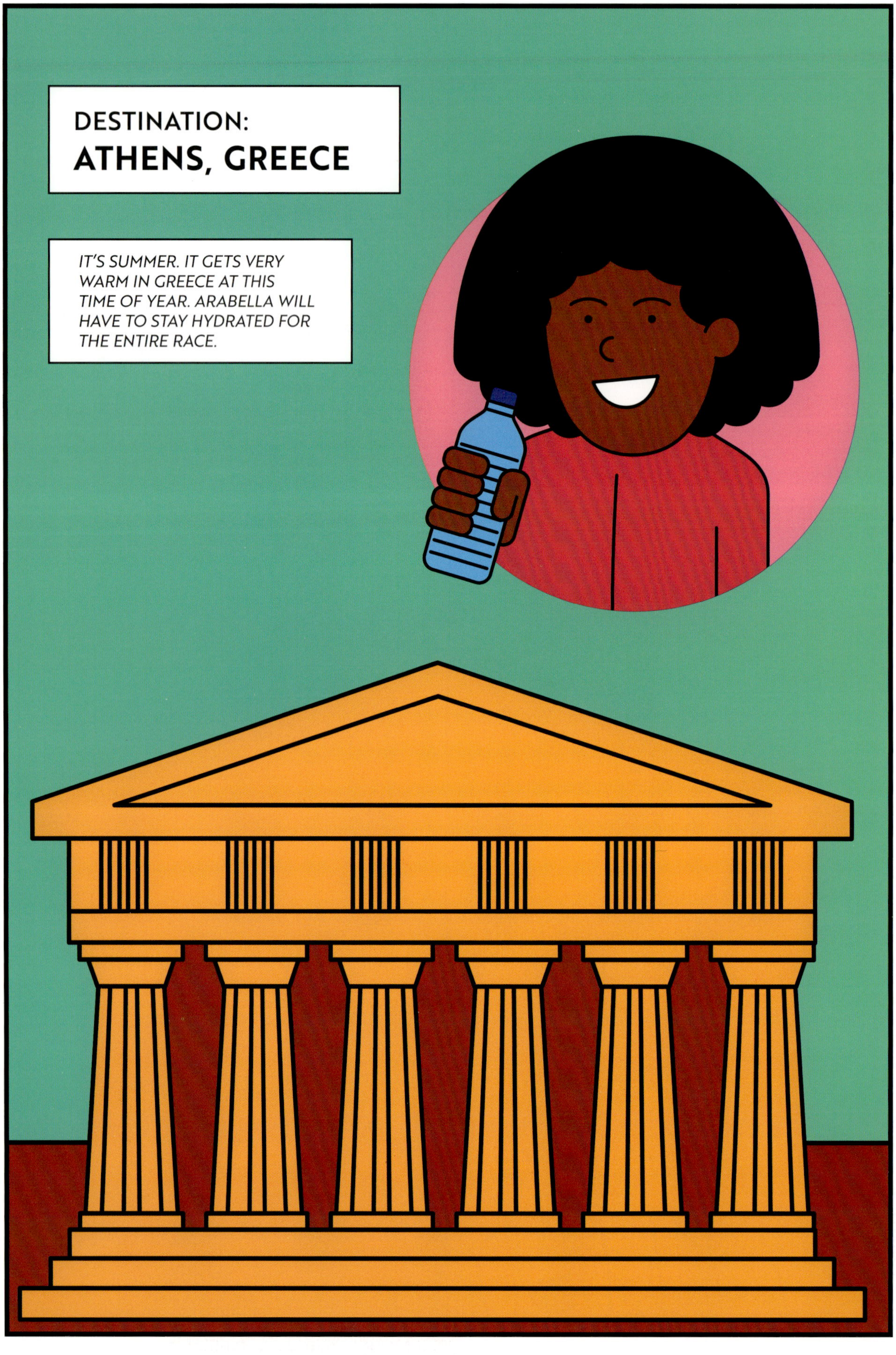
DESTINATION:
ATHENS, GREECE
IT'S SUMMER. IT GETS VERY WARM IN GREECE AT THIS TIME OF YEAR. ARABELLA WILL HAVE TO STAY HYDRATED FOR THE ENTIRE RACE.

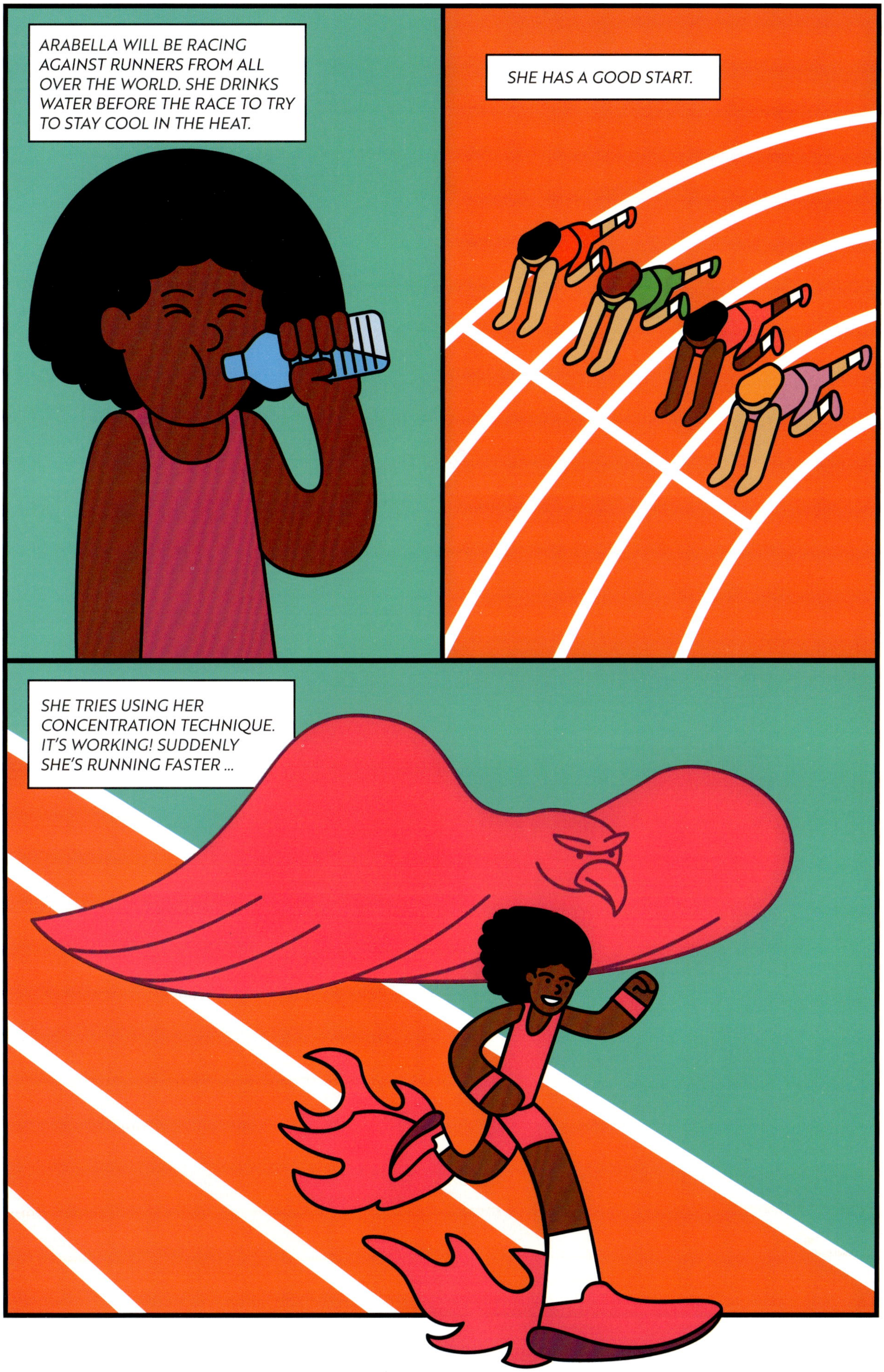
ARABELLA WILL BE RACING AGAINST RUNNERS FROM ALL OVER THE WORLD. SHE DRINKS WATER BEFORE THE RACE TO TRY TO STAY COOL IN THE HEAT.
SHE HAS A GOOD START.
SHE TRIES USING HER CONCENTRATION TECHNIQUE. IT'S WORKING! SUDDENLY SHE'S RUNNING FASTER ...

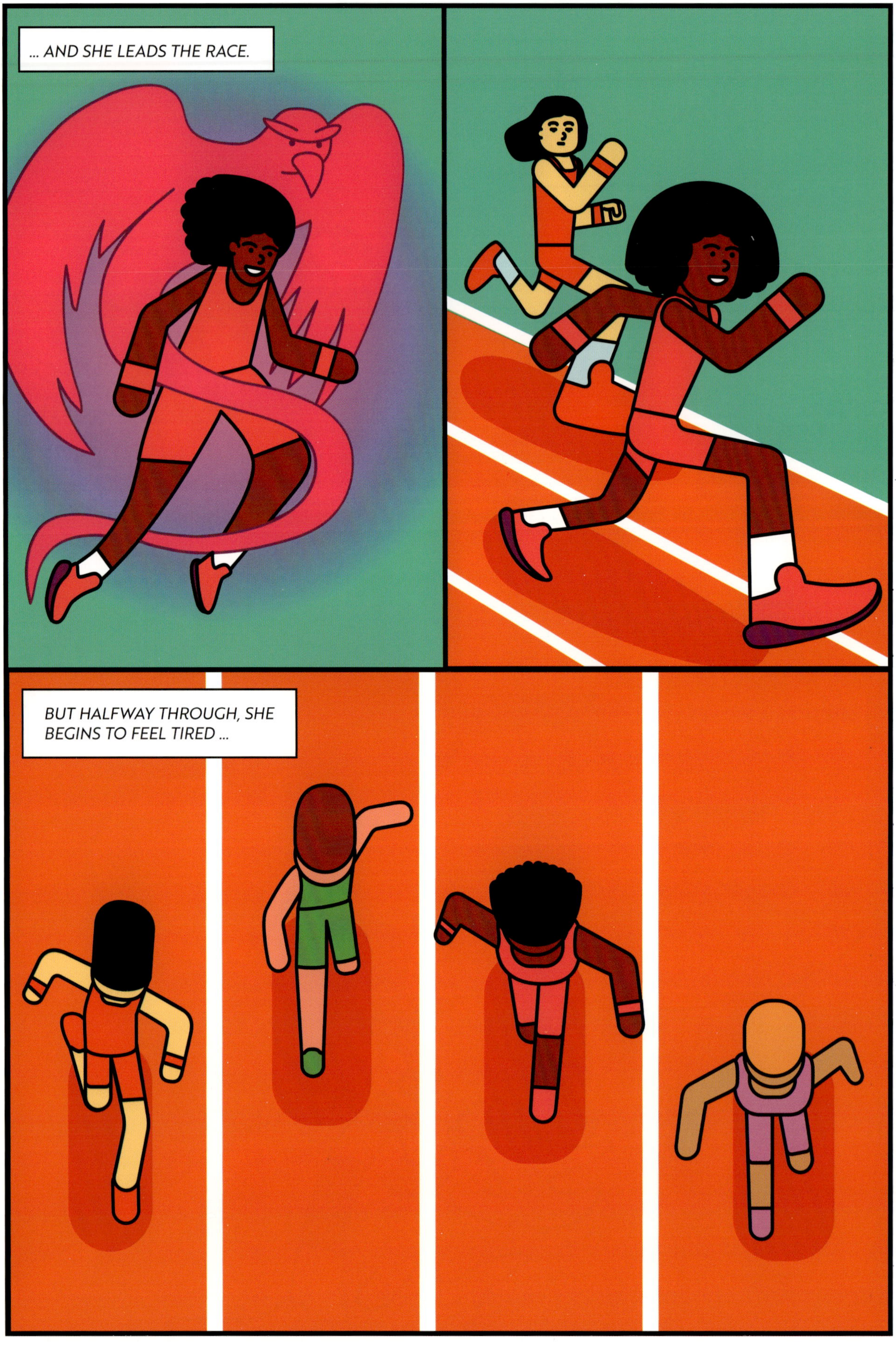
... AND SHE LEADS THE RACE.
BUT HALFWAY THROUGH, SHE BEGINS TO FEEL TIRED ...

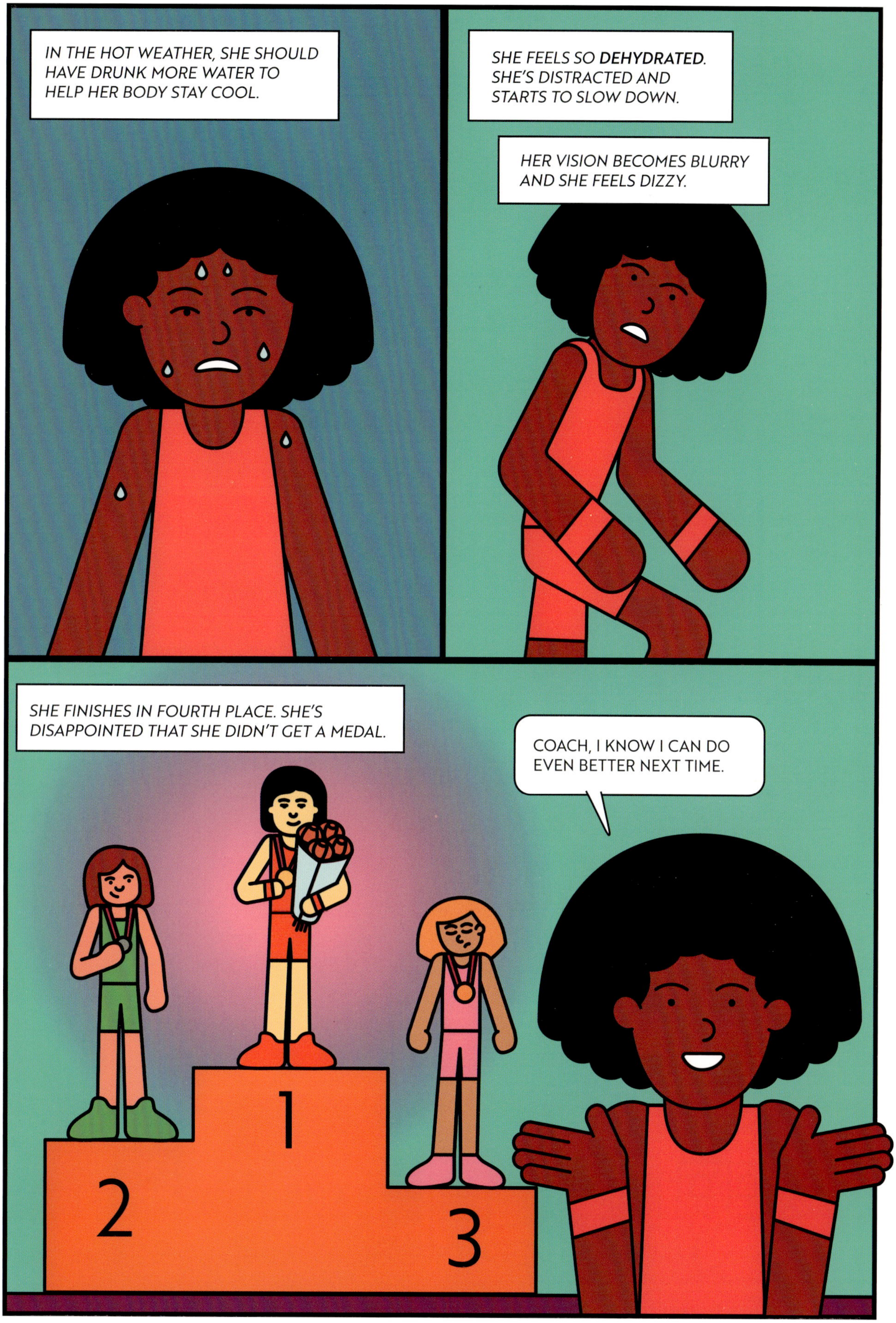
IN THE HOT WEATHER, SHE SHOULD HAVE DRUNK MORE WATER TO HELP HER BODY STAY COOL.
SHE FEELS SO **DEHYDRATED.** SHE'S DISTRACTED AND STARTS TO SLOW DOWN.
HER VISION BECOMES BLURRY AND SHE FEELS DIZZY.
SHE FINISHES IN FOURTH PLACE. SHE'S DISAPPOINTED THAT SHE DIDN'T GET A MEDAL.
COACH, I KNOW I CAN DO EVEN BETTER NEXT TIME.
2
1
3

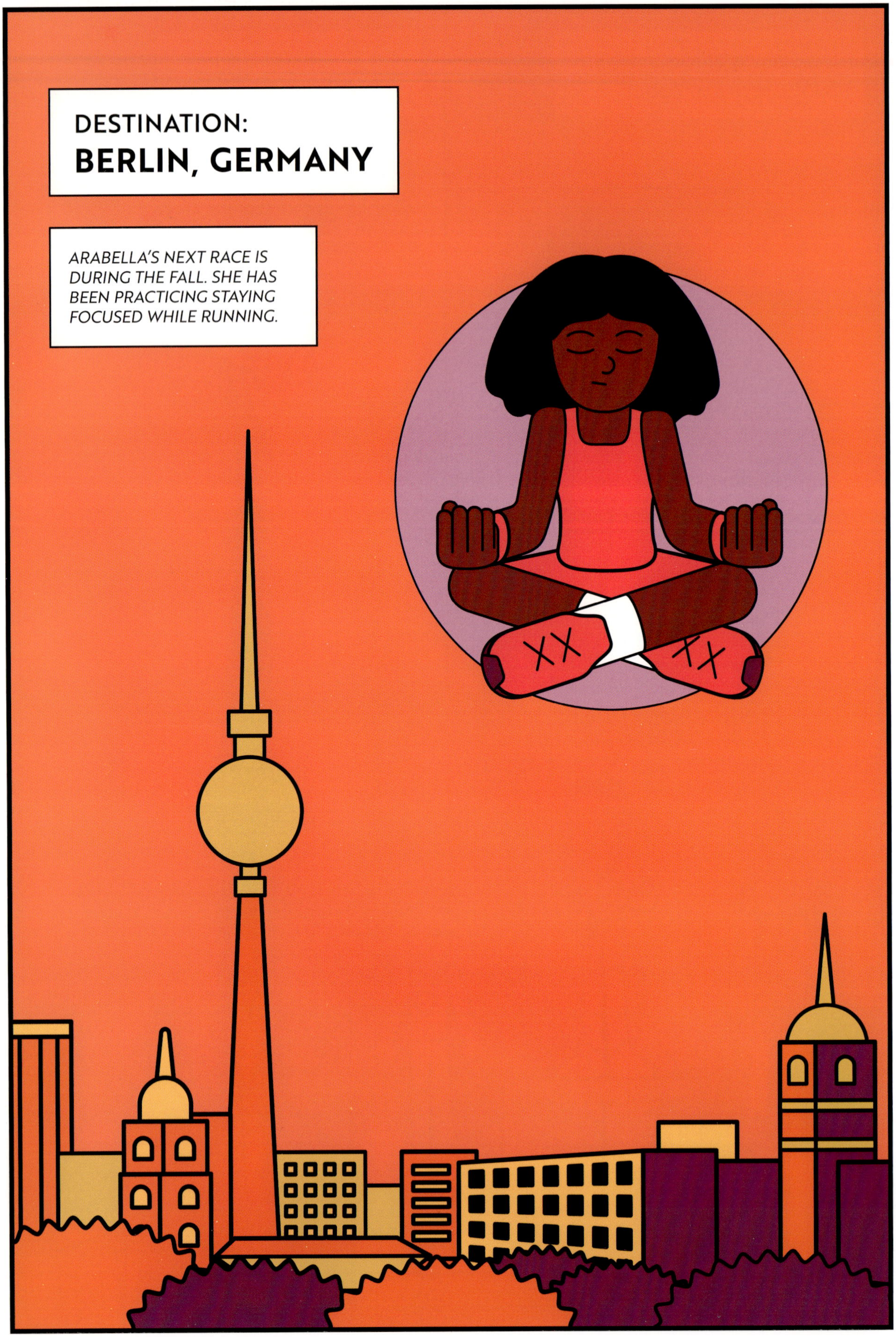
DESTINATION:
BERLIN, GERMANY
ARABELLA'S NEXT RACE IS DURING THE FALL. SHE HAS BEEN PRACTICING STAYING FOCUSED WHILE RUNNING.

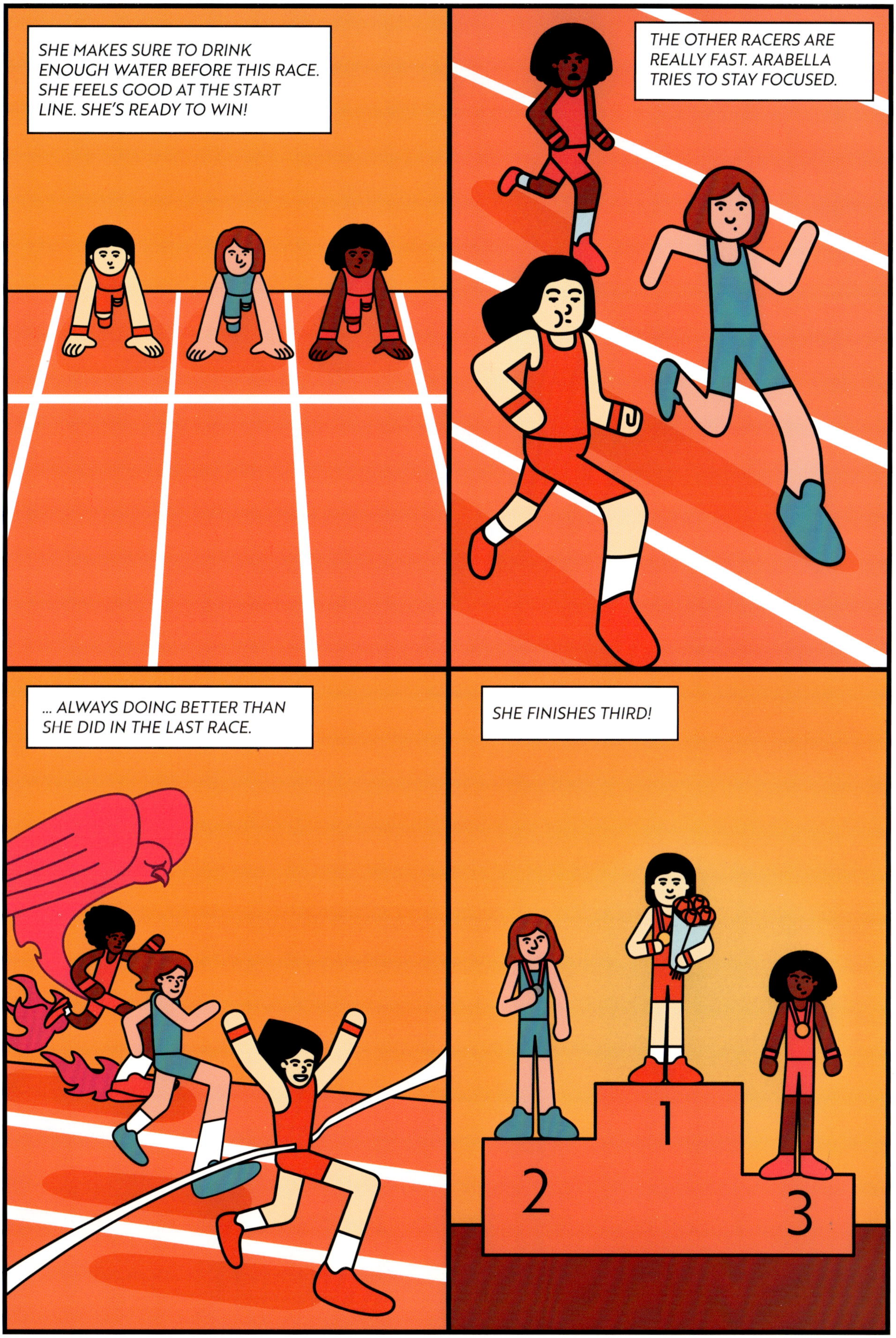
SHE MAKES SURE TO DRINK ENOUGH WATER BEFORE THIS RACE. SHE FEELS GOOD AT THE START LINE. SHE'S READY TO WIN!
THE OTHER RACERS ARE REALLY FAST. ARABELLA TRIES TO STAY FOCUSED.
... ALWAYS DOING BETTER THAN SHE DID IN THE LAST RACE.
SHE FINISHES THIRD!
1
2
3

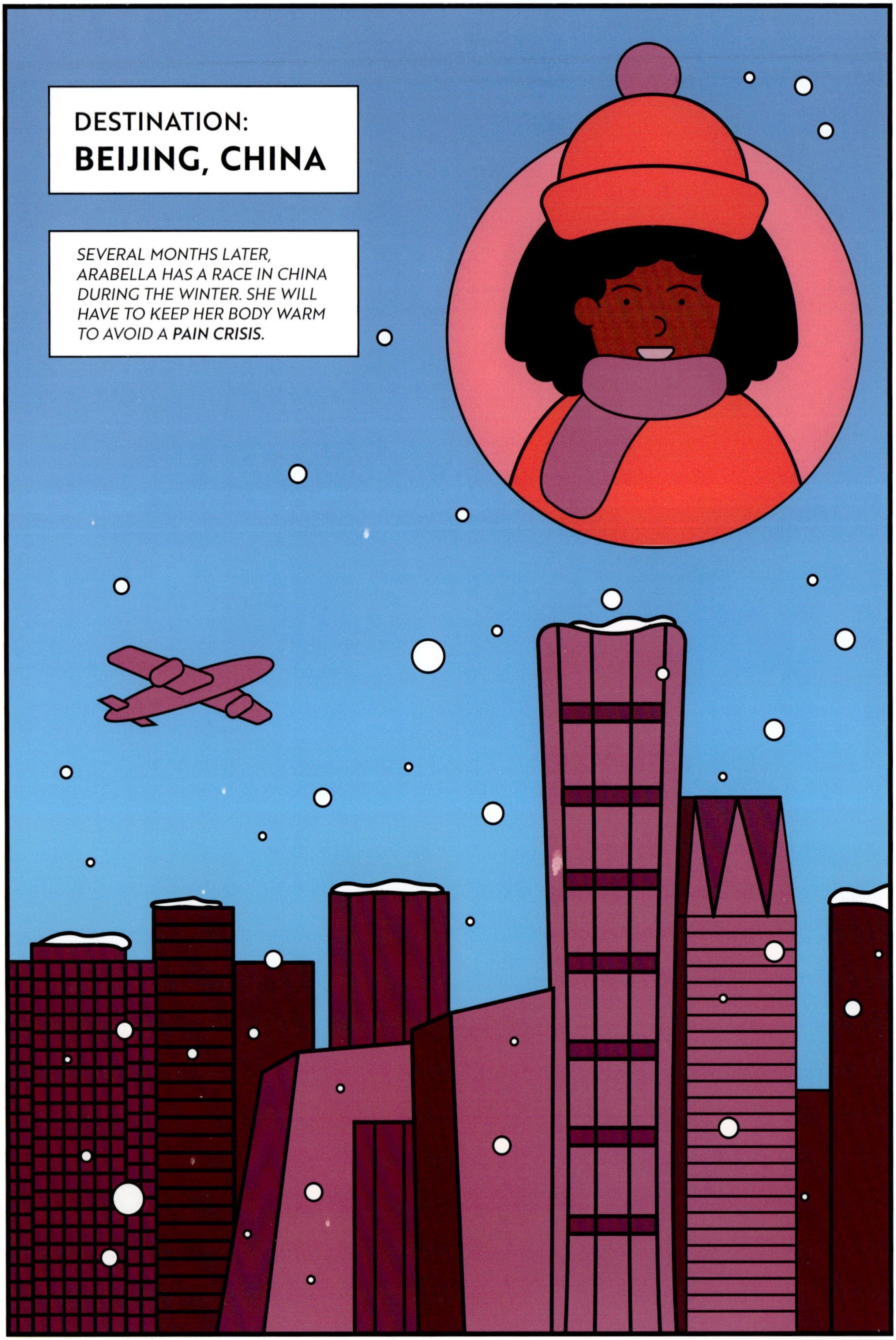
DESTINATION:
BEIJING, CHINA
SEVERAL MONTHS LATER, ARABELLA HAS A RACE IN CHINA DURING THE WINTER. SHE WILL HAVE TO KEEP HER BODY WARM TO AVOID A PAIN CRISIS.

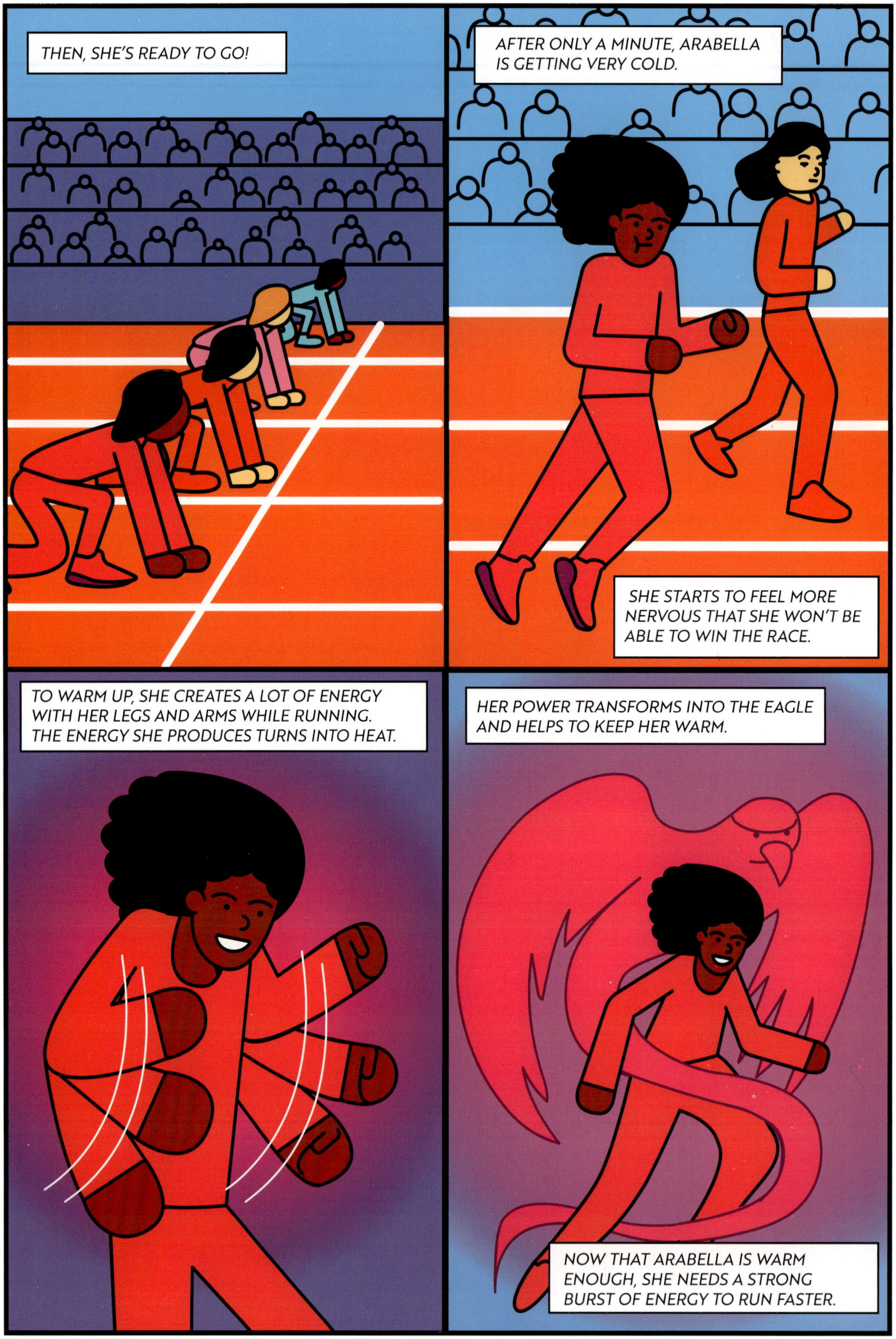
THEN, SHE'S READY TO GO!
AFTER ONLY A MINUTE, ARABELLA IS GETTING VERY COLD.
SHE STARTS TO FEEL MORE NERVOUS THAT SHE WON'T BE ABLE TO WIN THE RACE.
TO WARM UP, SHE CREATES A LOT OF ENERGY WITH HER LEGS AND ARMS WHILE RUNNING. THE ENERGY SHE PRODUCES TURNS INTO HEAT.
HER POWER TRANSFORMS INTO THE EAGLE AND HELPS TO KEEP HER WARM.
NOW THAT ARABELLA IS WARM ENOUGH, SHE NEEDS A STRONG BURST OF ENERGY TO RUN FASTER.

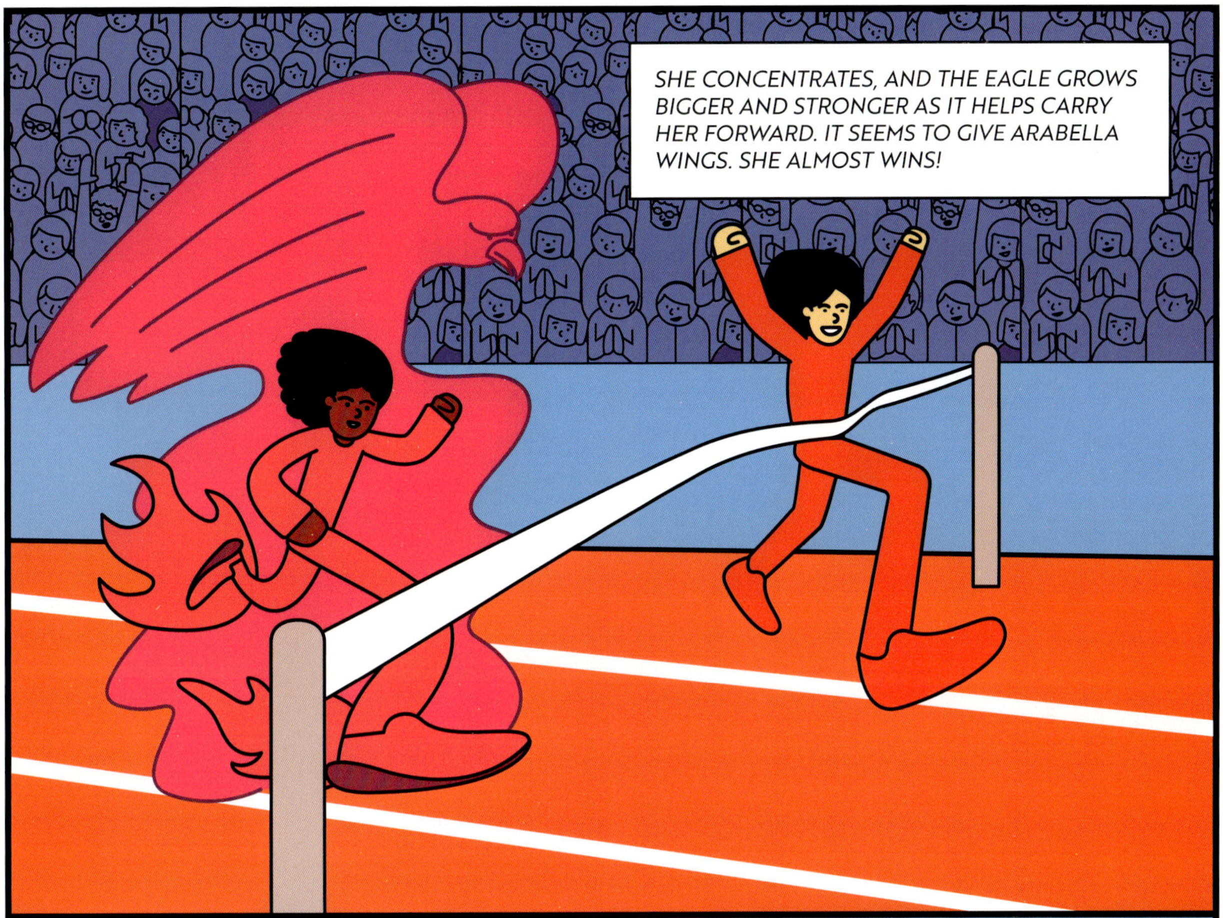
SHE CONCENTRATES, AND THE EAGLE GROWS BIGGER AND STRONGER AS IT HELPS CARRY HER FORWARD. IT SEEMS TO GIVE ARABELLA WINGS. SHE ALMOST WINS!

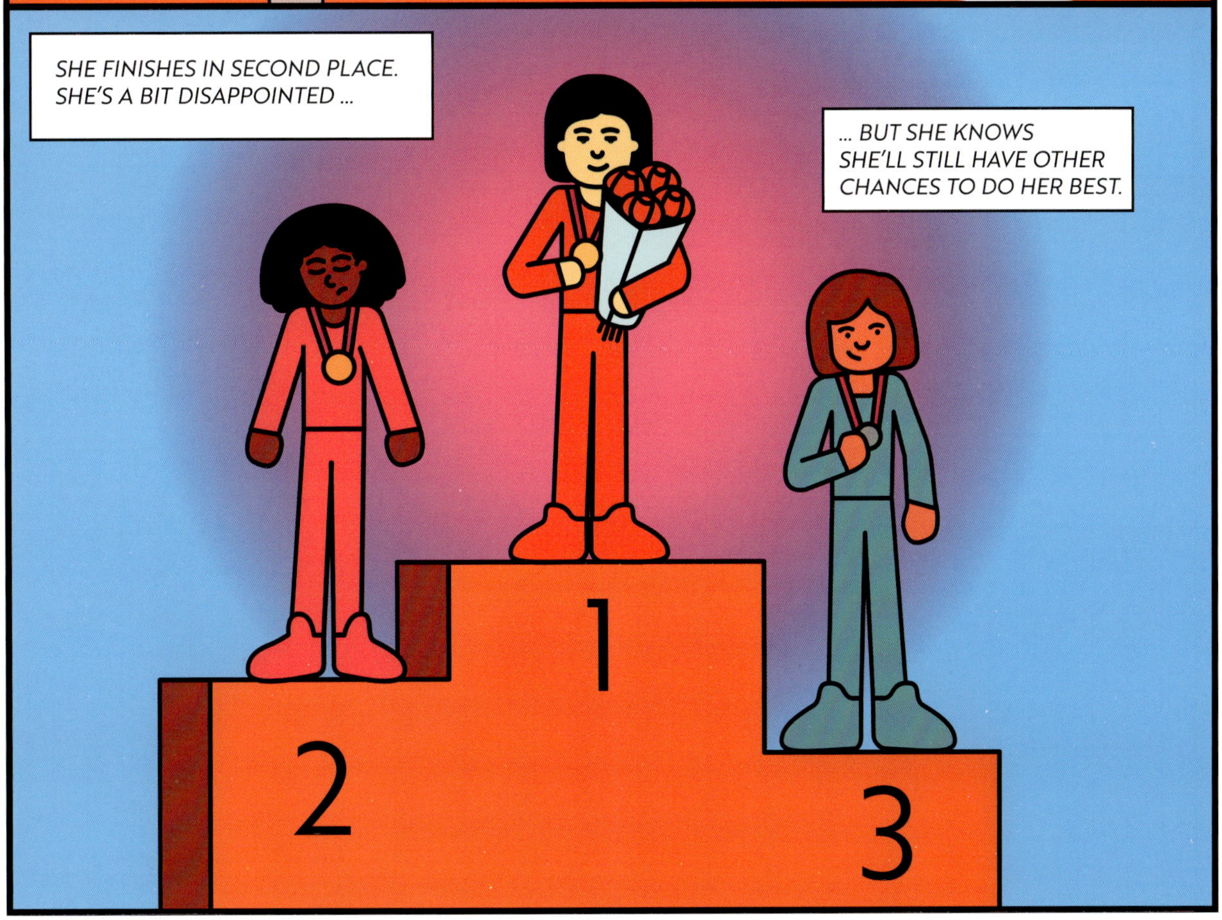
SHE FINISHES IN SECOND PLACE. SHE'S A BIT DISAPPOINTED ...
1
2
3
... BUT SHE KNOWS SHE'LL STILL HAVE OTHER CHANCES TO DO HER BEST.

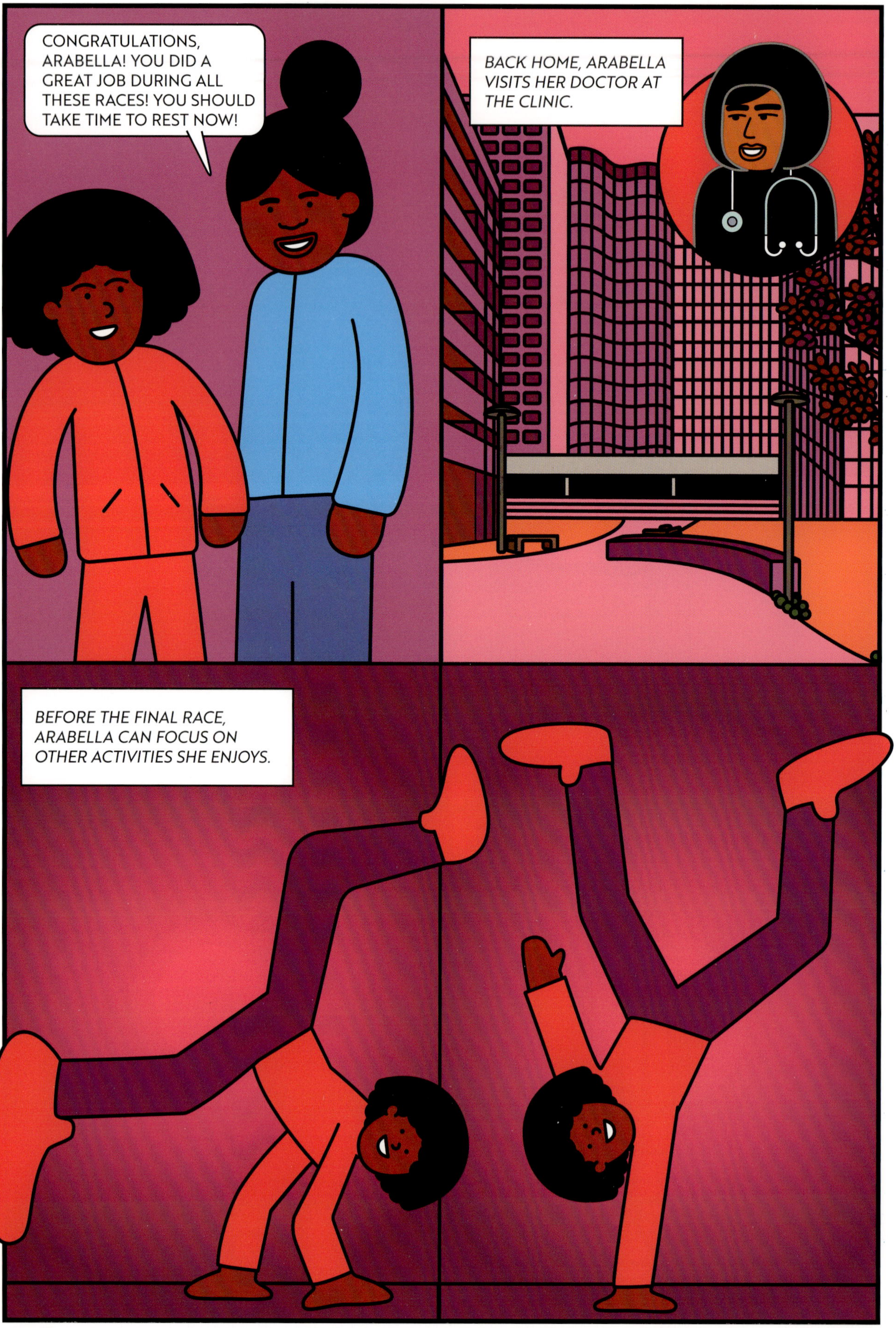
CONGRATULATIONS, ARABELLA! YOU DID A GREAT JOB DURING ALL THESE RACES! YOU SHOULD TAKE TIME TO REST NOW!
BACK HOME, ARABELLA VISITS HER DOCTOR AT THE CLINIC.
BEFORE THE FINAL RACE, ARABELLA CAN FOCUS ON OTHER ACTIVITIES SHE ENJOYS.

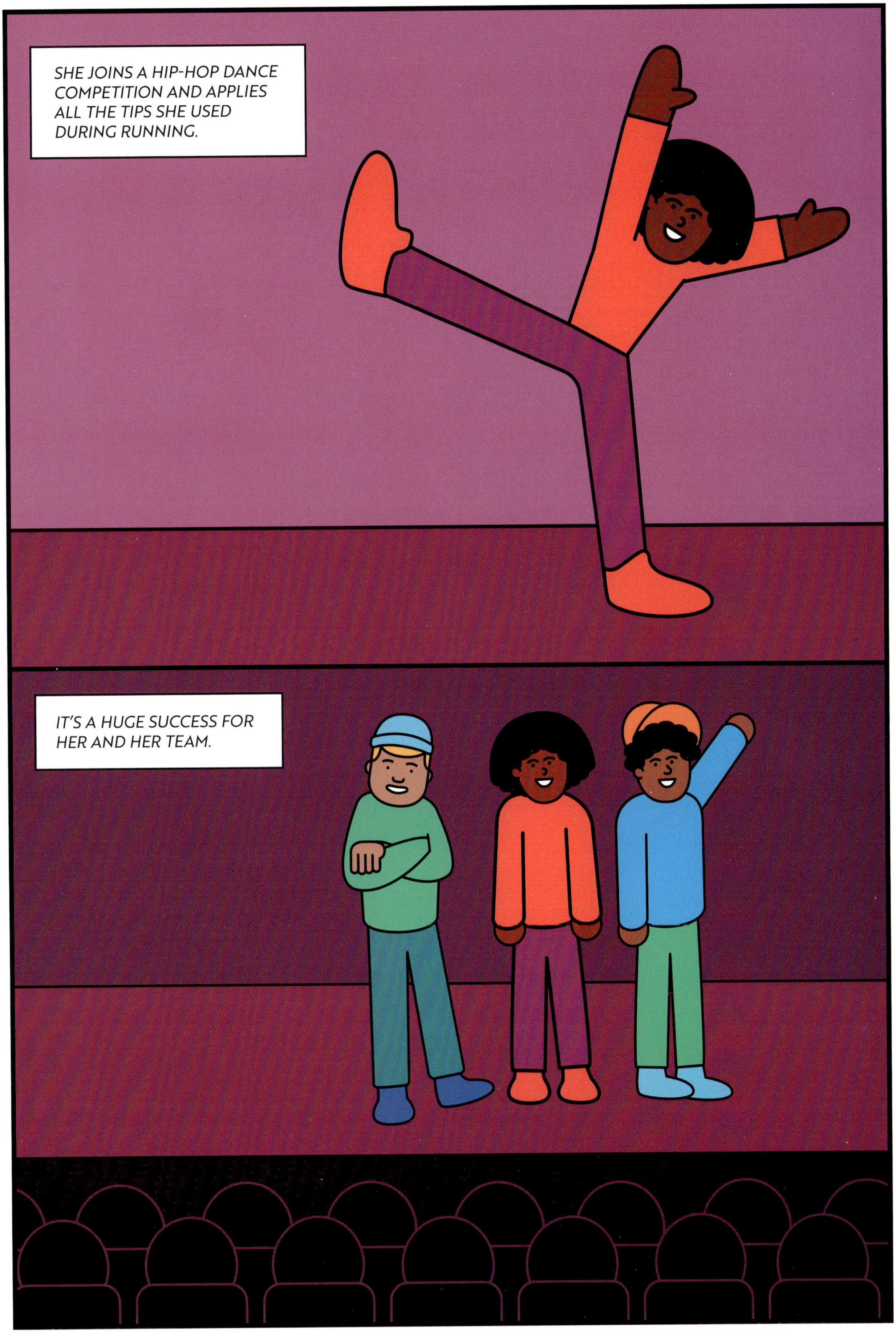
SHE JOINS A HIP-HOP DANCE COMPETITION AND APPLIES ALL THE TIPS SHE USED DURING RUNNING.
IT'S A HUGE SUCCESS FOR HER AND HER TEAM.

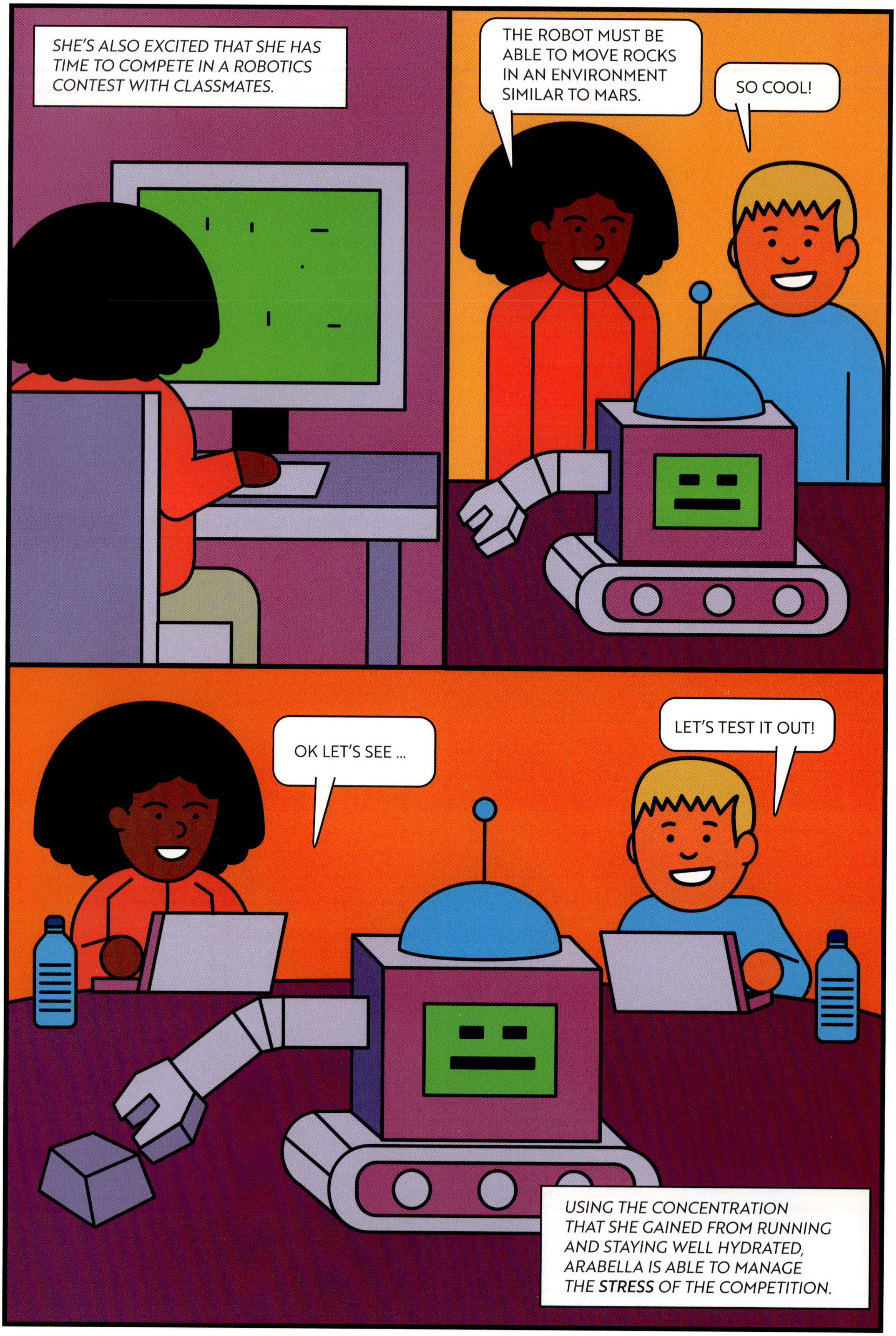
SHE'S ALSO EXCITED THAT SHE HAS TIME TO COMPETE IN A ROBOTICS CONTEST WITH CLASSMATES.
THE ROBOT MUST BE ABLE TO MOVE ROCKS IN AN ENVIRONMENT SIMILAR TO MARS.
SO COOL!
OK LET'S SEE ...
LET'S TEST IT OUT!
USING THE CONCENTRATION THAT SHE GAINED FROM RUNNING AND STAYING WELL HYDRATED, ARABELLA IS ABLE TO MANAGE THE **STRESS** OF THE COMPETITION.

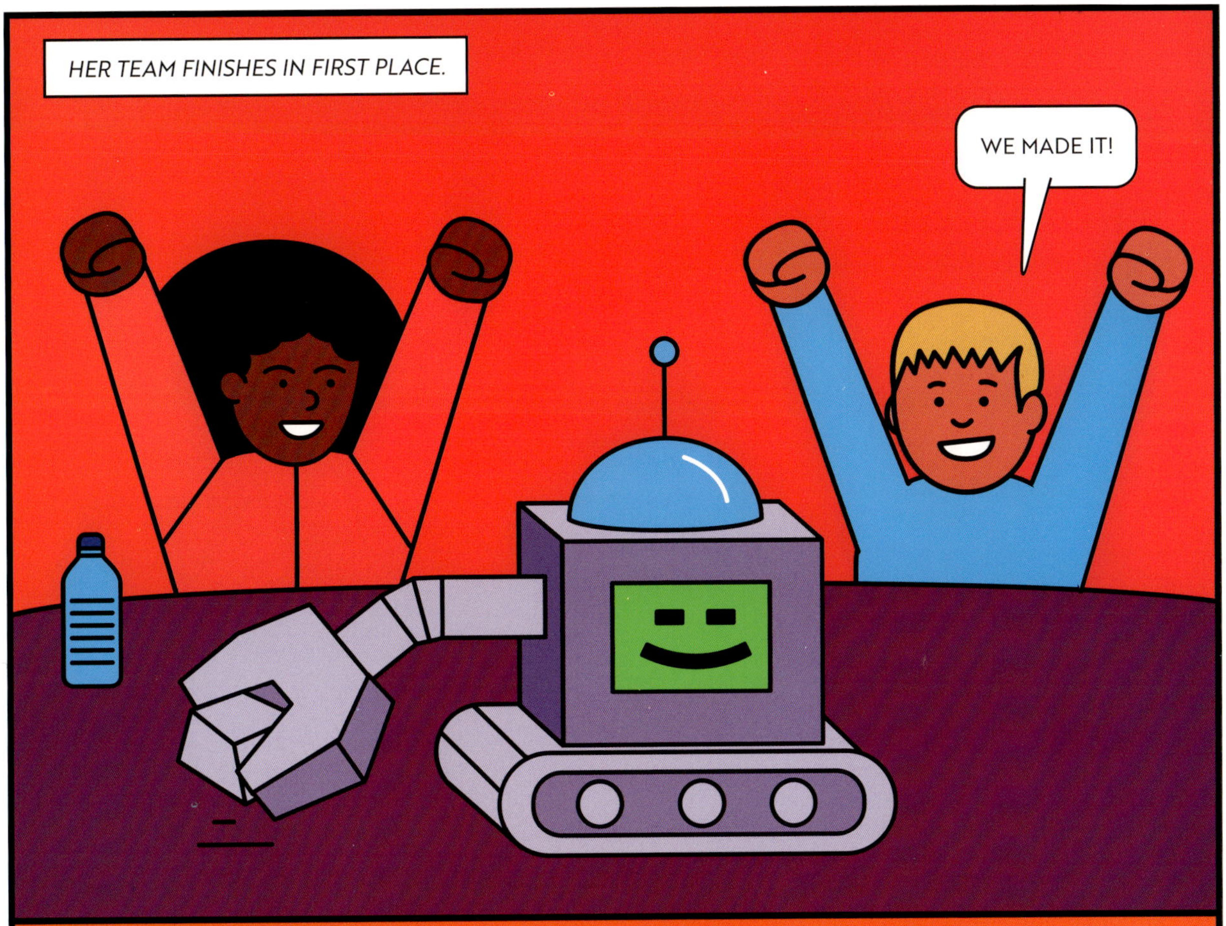
HER TEAM FINISHES IN FIRST PLACE.
WE MADE IT!

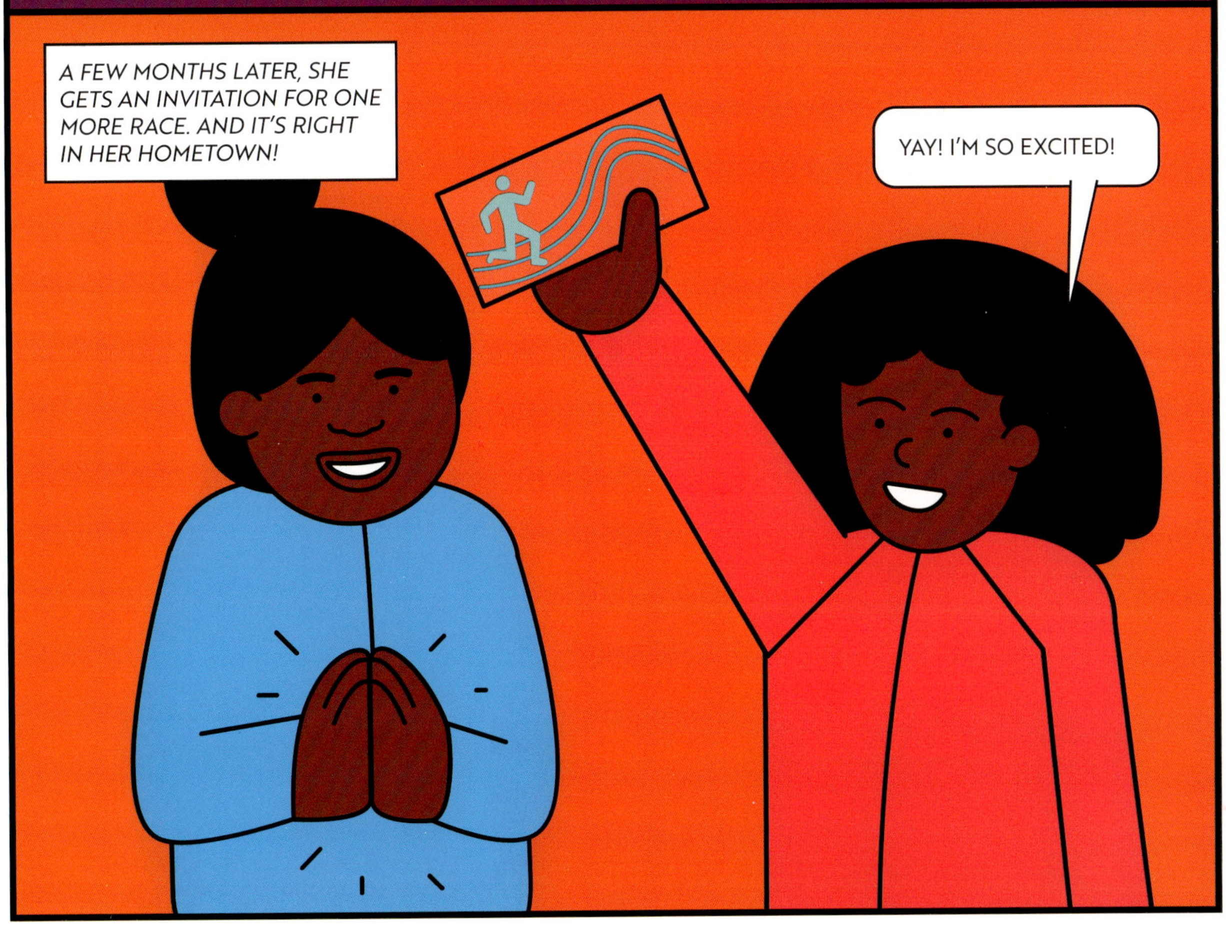
A FEW MONTHS LATER, SHE GETS AN INVITATION FOR ONE MORE RACE. AND IT'S RIGHT IN HER HOMETOWN!
YAY! I'M SO EXCITED!

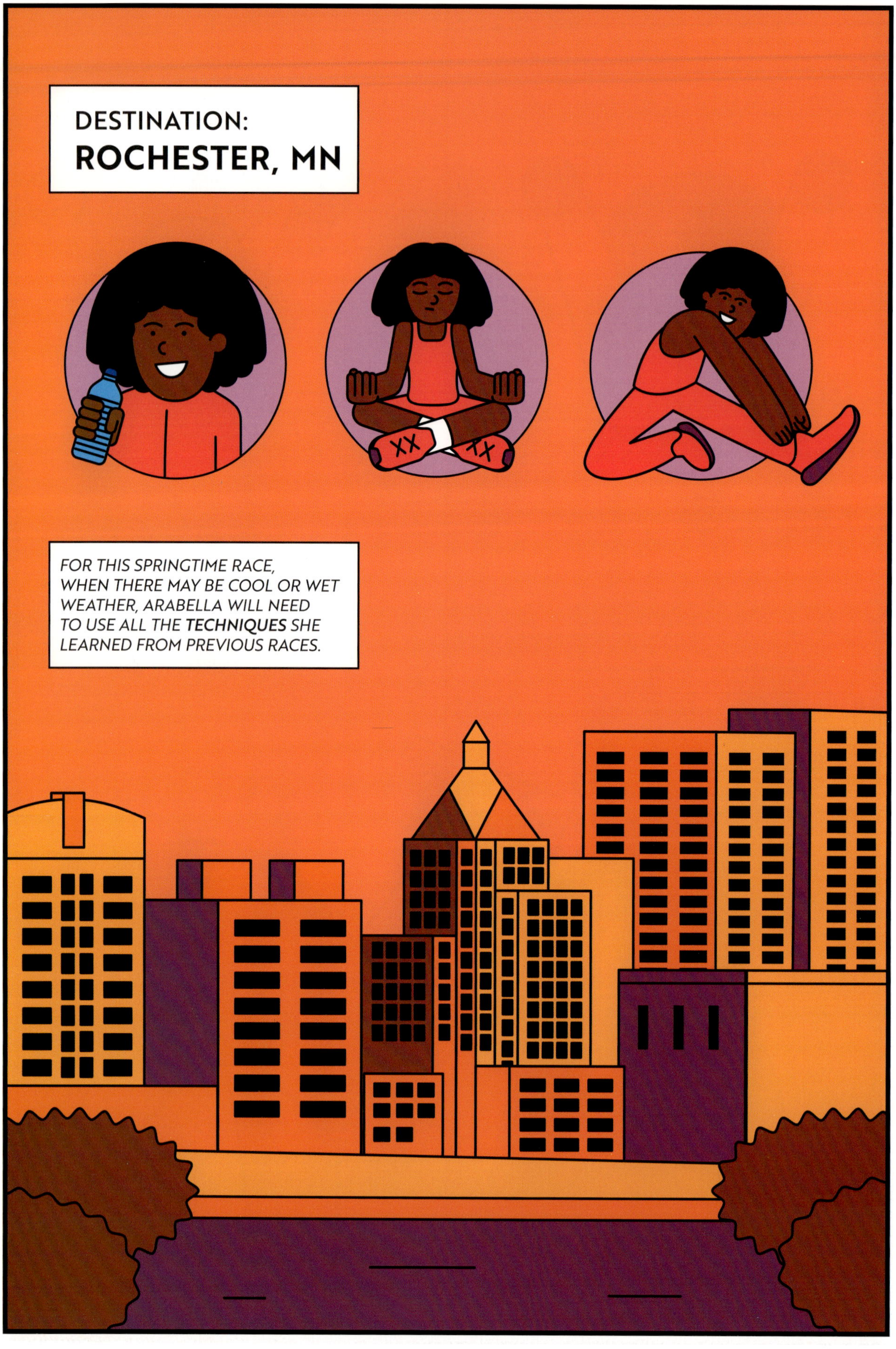
DESTINATION:
ROCHESTER, MN
FOR THIS SPRINGTIME RACE, WHEN THERE MAY BE COOL OR WET WEATHER, ARABELLA WILL NEED TO USE ALL THE **TECHNIQUES** SHE LEARNED FROM PREVIOUS RACES.

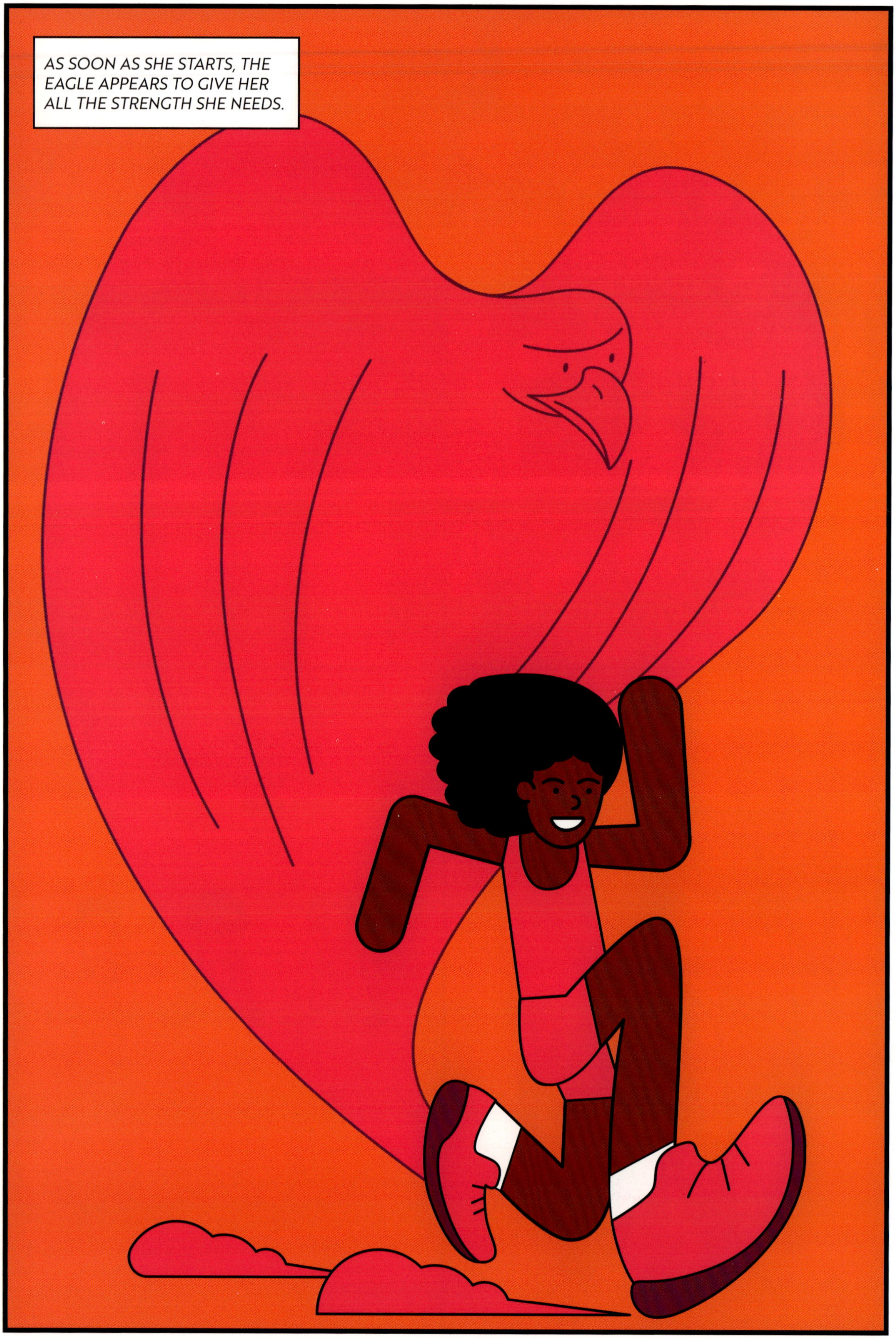
AS SOON AS SHE STARTS, THE EAGLE APPEARS TO GIVE HER ALL THE STRENGTH SHE NEEDS.

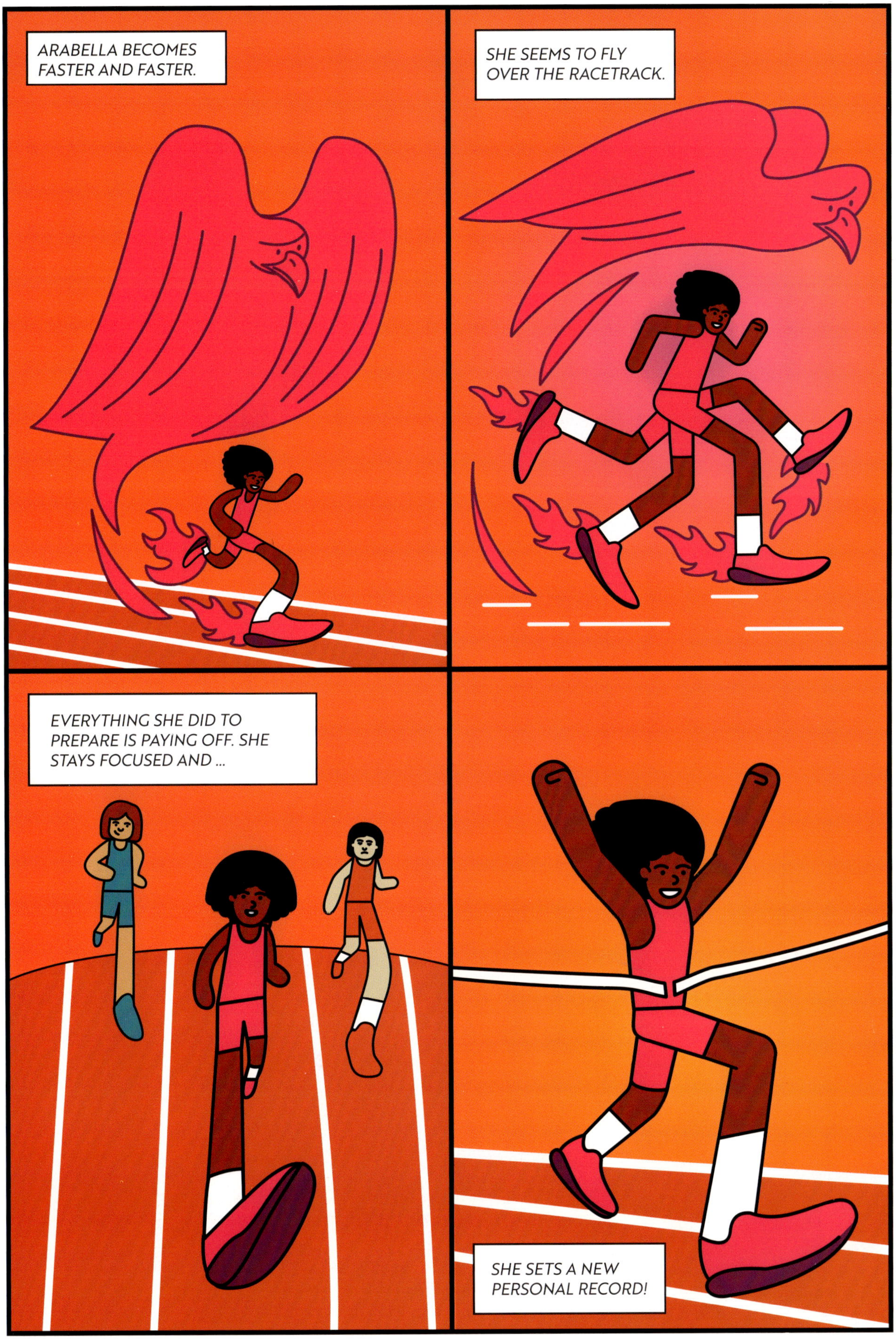
ARABELLA BECOMES FASTER AND FASTER.
SHE SEEMS TO FLY OVER THE RACETRACK.
EVERYTHING SHE DID TO PREPARE IS PAYING OFF. SHE STAYS FOCUSED AND ...
SHE SETS A NEW PERSONAL RECORD!

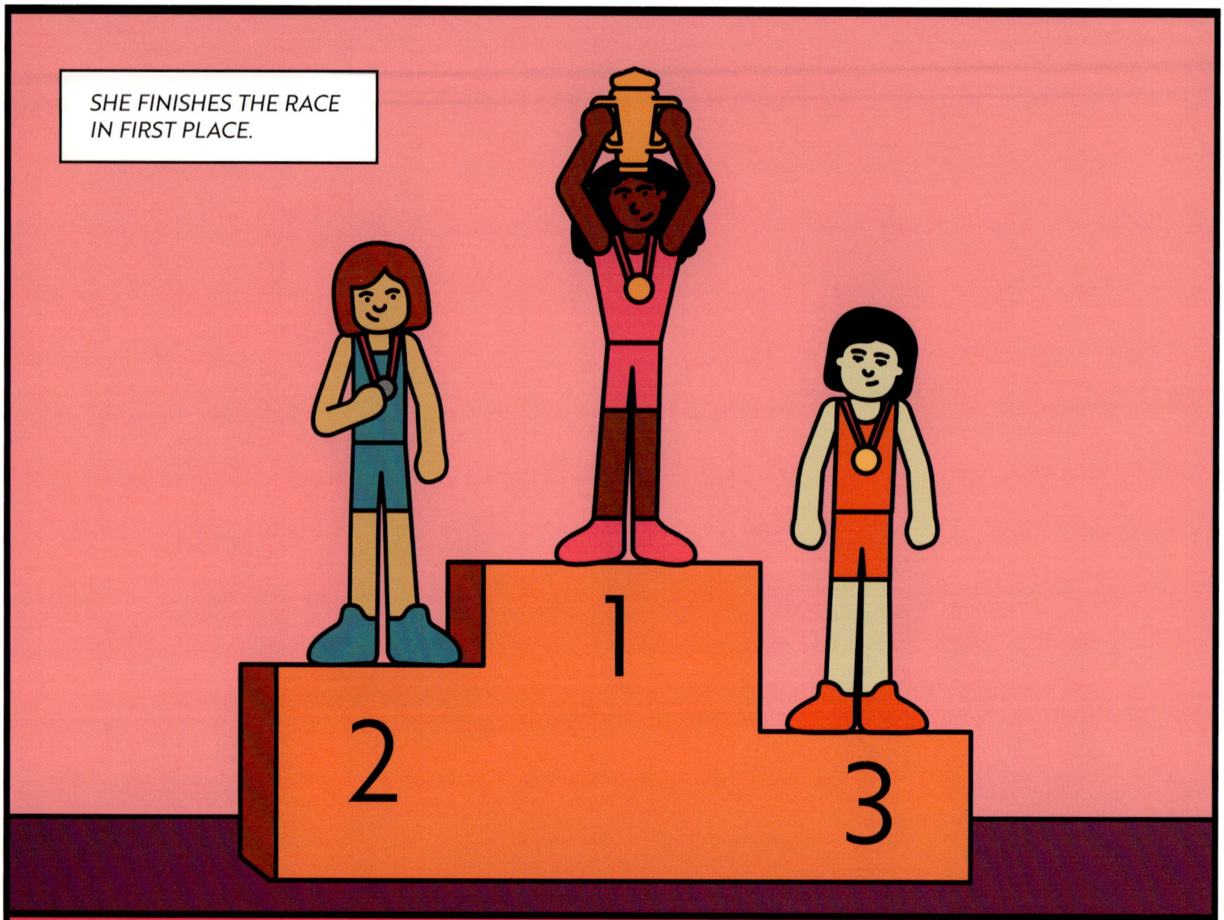
SHE FINISHES THE RACE IN FIRST PLACE.
2
1
3

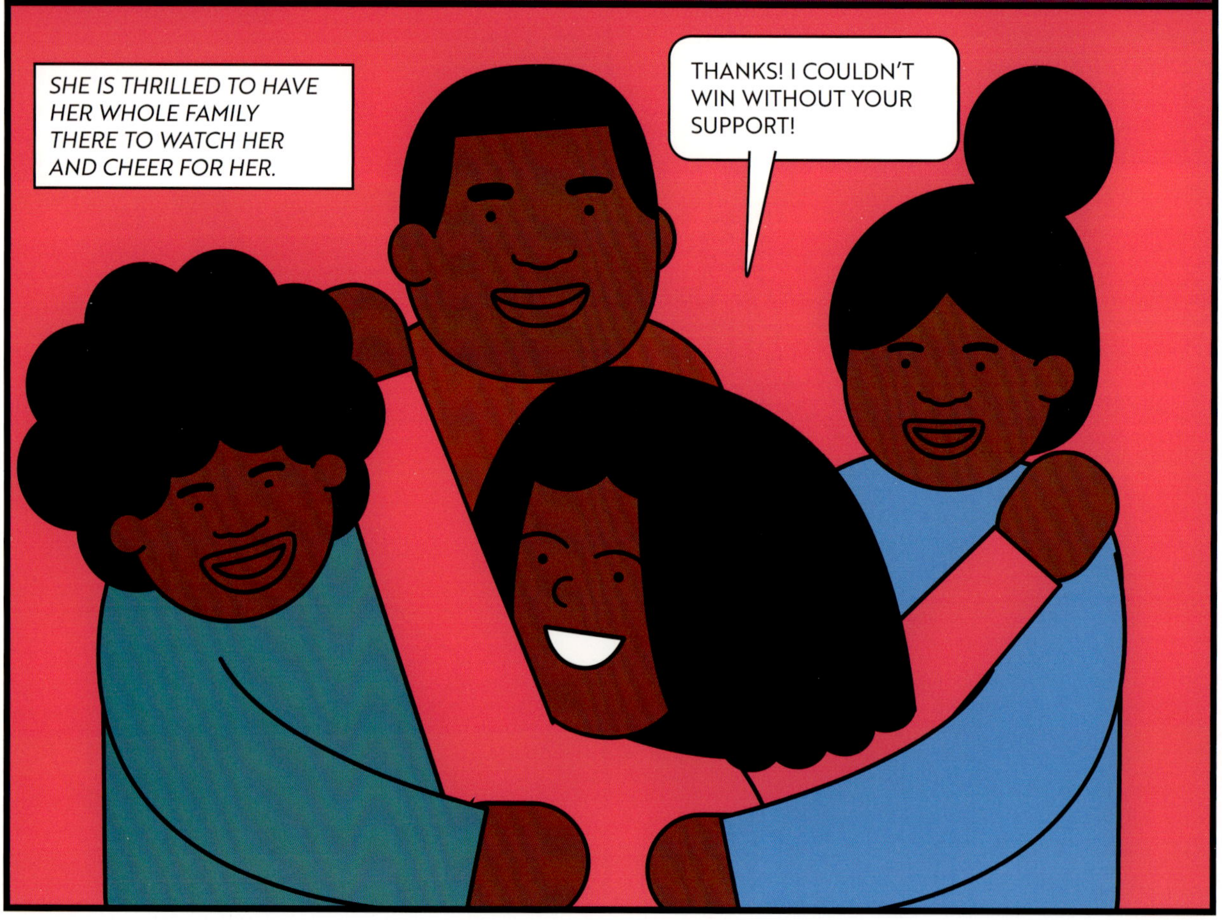
SHE IS THRILLED TO HAVE HER WHOLE FAMILY THERE TO WATCH HER AND CHEER FOR HER.
THANKS! I COULDN'T WIN WITHOUT YOUR SUPPORT!

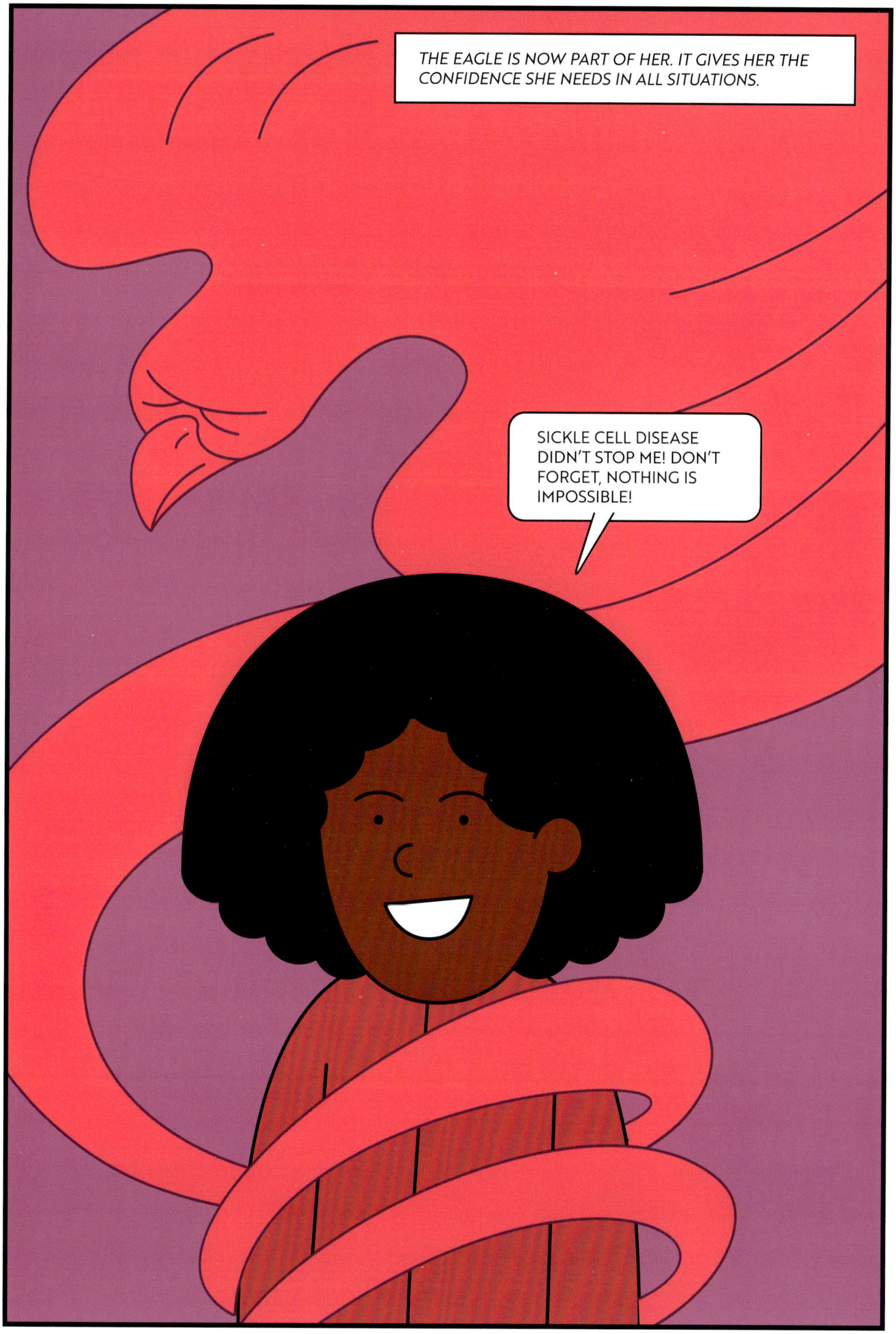
THE EAGLE IS NOW PART OF HER. IT GIVES HER THE CONFIDENCE SHE NEEDS IN ALL SITUATIONS.
SICKLE CELL DISEASE DIDN'T STOP ME! DON'T FORGET, NOTHING IS IMPOSSIBLE!

KEY TERMS

anemia: a condition in which you don't have enough healthy red blood cells to carry oxygen to your body's tissues. Having anemia can make you feel tired and weak.

dehydrated: when your body doesn't have enough water, other fluids and electrolytes to carry out its normal functions

genes: sections of your DNA, the code that controls much of your body's form and function. Genes are inside nearly every cell in your body. Genes that don't work properly can cause disease.

gene therapy: a treatment that replaces a gene, inactivates a gene or adds a new gene to cure disease or help your body fight disease

meditation: a type of mind-body medicine that involves deep focus. Meditation often focuses on the present moment, trying to limit random thoughts about the past or future.

pain crisis: a time of extreme pain caused by sickle cell anemia. Pain develops when sickle-shaped red blood cells block blood flow through tiny blood vessels to your chest, belly, limbs and joints.

red blood cells: cells that carry oxygen throughout the body

stress: an automatic physical, mental and emotional response to a challenging event

techniques: certain ways of managing a task or condition

MORE INFORMATION FROM THE MEDICAL EDITOR

By Asmaa Ferdjallah, M.D., M.P.H.
Senior Associate Consultant, Division of Pediatric Hematology/Oncology, Mayo Clinic, Rochester, MN; Assistant Professor of Pediatrics, Mayo Clinic College of Medicine and Science

Sickle cell disease is a disorder of the body's **red blood cells**. At any moment, trillions of **red blood cells** travel around the body. These cells carry oxygen from the lungs to muscles, organs and other tissues. Oxygen is used for energy to stay warm, build strength and keep the body's systems functioning. But with sickle cell disease, there are not enough healthy **red blood cells** to carry oxygen throughout the body.

Typically, **red blood cells** are flexible and round, and they move easily through blood vessels. In people who have sickle cell disease, some of these cells become sickle shaped, like crescent moons. They can easily get stuck in small blood vessels. This can slow or block the flow of blood and oxygen to parts of the body.

Sickle cell disease is more common among Black people than among people of other races. But anyone can have this condition. It is inherited, which means it passes from parents to children in the **genes**. A gene called HBB is linked to sickle cell disease. This gene tells the body how to make hemoglobin, a protein inside **red blood cells**. Hemoglobin carries oxygen to tissues. If the gene is changed, it's called a mutated gene. This means it doesn't work properly, and it can't create healthy **red blood cells**.

Both mother and father must pass on the changed HBB gene for their child to be affected. However, parents may carry the changed gene without being affected by the disease. In some families, both parents might be carriers of the changed gene but not have sickle cell disease. Or one parent may have the disease while the other parent carries the changed gene but is not affected. In either case, if both parents pass on the changed HBB gene, their child will have sickle cell disease. Newborn babies are now typically checked for this condition as part of standard health screenings.

Different types of sickle cell disease have different symptoms and complications. All types cause **anemia**. Anemia is a common blood disorder that occurs when a person does not have enough healthy **red blood cells** to carry oxygen throughout the body.

Signs and complications of sickle cell disease often appear around 5 months of age. However, some children may show signs or symptoms as early as 2 months old, with swollen fingers and hands. Every person is different. Some children have a variety of symptoms that may include pain, wheezing, trouble breathing, shortness of breath, belly pain and weakness. Others may not. In addition, signs and symptoms may be mild for some or life-threatening for others. Some symptoms may get better over time. Others may get worse or become severe.

The only cure for sickle cell disease is a bone marrow transplant or **gene therapy**. However, many treatments can reduce symptoms and help prevent complications. Many people with sickle cell disease take medications to help reduce pain crises, ease pain during a crisis, improve **anemia** and prevent infection. Medications that can help manage sickle cell disease include hydroxyurea, voxelotor and crizanlizumab. Scientists continue to work toward discovering more therapies.

REFERENCES

Brandow AM, et al. American Society of Hematology 2020 guidelines for sickle cell disease: management of acute and chronic pain. Blood Advances. 2020; doi: 10.1182/bloodadvances.2020001851.

WEB RESOURCES

Nemours KidsHealth — kidshealth.org
Search "sickle cell disease" on this site for information geared toward kids, teens or parents, including what to know about certain medications and tips for going away to college.

Sickle Cell Disease Coalition — www.scdcoalition.org
This coalition's site includes a variety of information and helpful tools for sickle cell disease, such as statistics, fact sheets for athletes and their coaches, and a directory of clinical trials.

Spark Sickle Cell Change — www.sparksicklecellchange.com
This resource for teens includes a medical explanation of sickle cell, a breakdown of the history of the condition, common barriers to care and tips for making your voice heard in a health care setting, as well as advice and stories from real people living with sickle cell.

Steps to Better Health for People with Sickle Cell Disease Toolkit — www.cdc.gov/ncbddd/sicklecell/betterhealthtoolkit/index.html
Find reader-friendly fact sheets on this page from the U.S. Centers for Disease Control and Prevention, with tips for common sickle cell disease complications, better heart health and more.

ABOUT THE MEDICAL EDITOR

Asmaa Ferdjallah, M.D., M.P.H.
Senior Associate Consultant, Division of Pediatric Hematology/Oncology, Mayo Clinic, Rochester, MN; Assistant Professor of Pediatrics, Mayo Clinic College of Medicine and Science

Dr. Ferdjallah is a pediatric hematologist and bone marrow transplant physician with expertise in sickle cell disease and thalassemia. She envisions a clinical care model where all people with sickle cell disease are cared for by a hematologist with training in bone marrow transplant so that curative therapy can be started sooner. She is also interested in global health, both locally and internationally, and is passionate about optimizing care for people with language or cultural barriers. She strives to set a great example for learners and is passionate about medical education.

ABOUT THE AUTHORS

Guillaume Federighi, aka **Hey Gee**, is a French and American author and illustrator. He began his career in 1998 in Paris, France. He also spent a few decades exploring the world of street art and graffiti in different European capitals. After moving to New York in 2008, he worked with many companies and brands, developing a reputation in graphic design and illustration for his distinctive style of translating complex ideas into simple and timeless visual stories.
He is also the owner and creative director of Hey Gee Studio, a full-service creative agency based in New York City.

Golden Ella was born in Rochester, Minnesota. She enjoys sports, riding her scooter, doing track and field, singing in the honors choir, performing in plays, getting rambunctious with her dog, Samson, and bossing her younger brother around. She became ill at 9 months old and stopped crawling and walking, due to a life-threatening case of osteomyelitis, an infection of the hip and pelvic bones, caused by sickle cell disease. Always a fighter, she worked her way to recovery through surgery, infusions and the medication hydroxyurea. She also credits dedicated care from her health care providers and love and support from her mom, dad, two older sisters, an older brother and a younger brother. She is determined to become a pediatrician focused on hematology and oncology to help other children like her and to find a cure for sickle cell disease.

ABOUT FONDATION IPSEN BOOKLAB

At the service of the general interest, working toward an equitable society, the Fondation Ipsen BookLab publishes and distributes books free of charge, primarily to schools and associations. Through collaborations between experts, artists, authors and children, our publications, for all ages and in a variety of languages, focus on the education and awareness of issues related to health, disability and rare diseases. Discover our complete catalog online at www.fondation-ipsen.org/book-lab.

ABOUT MAYO CLINIC PRESS

Launched in 2019, Mayo Clinic Press shines a light on the most fascinating stories in medicine and empowers individuals with the knowledge to build healthier, happier lives. From the award-winning *Mayo Clinic Health Letter* to books and media covering the scope of human health and wellness, Mayo Clinic Press publications provide readers with reliable and trusted content by some of the world's leading health care professionals. Proceeds benefit important medical research and education at Mayo Clinic. For more information about Mayo Clinic Press, visit MCPress.MayoClinic.org.

ABOUT THE COLLABORATION

The My Life Beyond series was developed in partnership between Fondation Ipsen's BookLab and Mayo Clinic, which has provided world-class medical education for more than 150 years. This collaboration aims to provide trustworthy, impactful resources for understanding childhood diseases and other problems that can affect children's well-being.

The series offers readers a holistic perspective of children's lives with — and beyond — their medical challenges. In creating these books, young people who have been Mayo Clinic patients worked together with author-illustrator Hey Gee, sharing their personal experiences. The resulting fictionalized stories authentically bring to life the patients' emotions and their inspiring responses to challenging circumstances. In addition, Mayo Clinic physicians contributed the latest medical expertise on each topic so that these stories can best help other patients, families and caregivers understand how children perceive and work through their own challenges.

Text: Hey Gee and Golden Ella
Illustrations: Hey Gee

Medical editor: Asmaa Ferdjallah, M.D., M.P.H., Senior Associate Consultant, Division of Pediatric Hematology/Oncology, Mayo Clinic, Rochester, MN; Assistant Professor of Pediatrics, Mayo Clinic College of Medicine and Science

Managing editor: Anna Cavallo, Health Education and Content Services/Mayo Clinic Press, Mayo Clinic, Rochester, MN
Project manager: Kim Chandler, Department of Education, Mayo Clinic, Rochester, MN
Manager of publications: Céline Colombier-Maffre, Fondation Ipsen, Paris, France
President: James A. Levine, M.D., Ph.D., Professor, Fondation Ipsen, Paris, France

MAYO CLINIC PRESS KIDS
200 First St. SW
Rochester, MN 55905
mcpress.mayoclinic.org

© 2023 Mayo Foundation for Medical Education and Research (MFMER)

MAYO, MAYO CLINIC and the Mayo triple-shield logo are marks of Mayo Foundation for Medical Education and Research. Published by Mayo Clinic Press Kids, an imprint of Mayo Clinic Press. All rights reserved. No part of this book may be reproduced, stored in a retrieval system, or transmitted, in any form or by any means, electronic, mechanical, photocopying, recording or otherwise, without the prior written permission of the publisher.

The information in this book is true and complete to the best of our knowledge. This book is intended only as an informative guide for those wishing to learn more about health issues. It is not intended to replace, countermand or conflict with advice given to you by your own physician. The ultimate decision concerning your care should be made between you and your doctor. Information in this book is offered with no guarantees. The author and publisher disclaim all liability in connection with the use of this book.

ISBN: 978-1-945564-65-9 (HC); 978-1-945564-66-6 (ePub)

Library of Congress Control Number 2022942498

Printed in the United States of America